BLACKWOOD YESTERDAY

in photographs
including the villages of
CWMFELINFACH, YNYSDDU, PONTLLANFRAITH,
OAKDALE, CEFN FFOREST, FLEUR-DE-LYS,
ABERBARGOED, ARGOED,
AND MARKHAM

Ewart Smith, M.Sc.

Foreword by
Edward J. Maguire,
B.A., Dip. Ed., FRGS

Book 4

Old Bakehouse Publications

Abertillery

First published in September 2001

ISBN 1 874538 29 8

Published in the U.K. by
Old Bakehouse Publications
Church Street,
Abertillery, Gwent NP13 1EA
Telephone: 01495 212600 Fax: 01495 216222
www.mediamaster.co.uk/oldbakebooks

Made and printed in the UK
by J.R. Davies (Printers) Ltd.

Foreword

by
Edward J. Maguire B.A., Dip. Ed., FRGS
former Headmaster of Pontllanfraith Comprehensive School
Past District Governor of Rotary International

In the 1820s as Blackwood was beginning its life as a settlement, the poet Coleridge was writing his *'Biographia Literaria'* and commenting on *'Memory emancipated from the order of time and place'*. **Blackwood Yesterday Book 4** contains a kaleidoscopic collection of memories from our past. Once again Ewart Smith has rescued from *'that great dust heap called History'* impressions of the past through photographs and words. Our older readers will wallow in the pleasures of nostalgia as the pages of this book are turned. Some photographs will evoke thoughts of childhood like apparitions coming through the mists of time. Idiosyncratic events triggered by a picture of a school group; a rugby team; a choir; an outing; or even a building will bring a smile to the lips - a tear to the eye. Those emotional memories immured in the back of our minds are re-kindled by this splendid collection of photographs. For younger readers, whose *'Blackwood Yesterdays'* are not personalised history, there is so much in this volume which will help characterise the past. Surely, they will be intrigued by the quaintness and peculiarities of events a mere speck of time ago. Perhaps, too, as they relate to this record of less than two hundred years of our local history they will appreciate how fortunate we are today. The chapter on *'The Early Days'* brings out the harsh realities of life in the early 1800s. School log books; gravestones records; the lot of the *'unpaid housewife'* reflect conditions none of us would wish to see again.

In shaping the future no community can afford to abandon the heritage of its past. Ewart Smith in his series of books on *'Blackwood Yesterday'* is reminding us about the nature of that heritage, and ensuring that a record is left which is entertaining as well as instructive

Eddie Maguire

Contents

CHAPTER 1
The Early Days

No significant event took place in Blackwood until the nineteenth century. We can't go back very far; not like Chepstow or Monmouth. Although the Sirhowy ironworks was working in the 1770s there was nothing in Blackwood until the tramroad was opened in 1805. The population of Bedwellty parish, which included the ironworks at the northern end of the Sirhowy Valley, grew from 1434 in 1801 to 22,413 in 1841. Blackwood, the only colliery town in the area, began life in 1820; it was planned as a model garden village by John Moggridge, industrialist, philanthropist, and a former friend of John Frost. By 1829 Blackwood had 100 inhabitants and as it continued to grow it acquired a reputation for having the worst sanitation and drainage in the county. The town, which supplied a lot of coal to Newport, was soon as black and overcrowded as any of the iron towns to the north.

Jobs were often insecure, wages low, and food prices high. As a consequence many children did not go to school; it was often more important to have another wage earner in the family. The poorer the family, the earlier the children began to work. In the early 1800s in the vicinity of Blackwood, school buildings and attendance were poor and Tremenheere, the Government Commissioner, estimated that two-thirds of the working class children received no formal education whatsoever. Think for a moment of what it was like to live in Blackwood in those days: no electricity - so no electric lights, television, heating, washing machines, cleaners or power tools -, no mains water, no mains toilets, no toilet paper, no cars, buses or trains, no street lighting, no tarmac roads, little or no food from abroad for the common man and no modern medicine. Life expectancy for the period from 1790 to 1830, as indicated by the gravestones in Bedwellty churchyard, was less than 30 years; one child in four did not reach his/her 10th birthday! What did people do with their time apart from work? Not a lot, but when there was leisure time it was spent either in the ale house, which meant beer, cards, billiards, the dice box and skittles; or in the chapels and churches. The coal owners were predominantly English and members of the Church of England. The workers believed they were being exploited and wanted to get away from their employers as often as they could. This may be the prime reason that the nonconformist churches and chapels thrived so well in this area.

Around 1830 a Monmouthshire Friendly Society of Coal Mining was formed. Its main objectives were to prevent newcomers being taught the art of mining and to protect the interests of its members by obtaining the highest possible wages and by limiting output. Members of the Society were not permitted to take newcomers underground unless they were the children of members. If the owners decided to employ extra labour underground, the newcomers were expected to pay a sum to the Society's nearest branch before they could be employed. The Society sent delegates to Bolton in 1831 and, as a result, joined the National Society for the Protection of Labour. The ironmasters and coalowners then gave notice that no 'union' men would be employed in future. Many were locked out because they would not sign a document which said that they were not members of a *'union'*. As a result the *'union'* went underground and an organisation that became known as Scotch Cattle began to operate. Why it was called Scotch Cattle is not obvious. A dictionary tells us that to scotch means *'to render such hurt on a person or thing as to make it temporarily harmless, to crush, to stamp out'*. Cattle may have been used because of the emblem of the group - a bull's head with horns. We still talk about *'scotching a rumour'*. Its reputed leader was a man called Ned who had come to this area from Staffordshire. Members of the Scotch Cattle were believed to be connected in some way with almost every strike or disturbance in the coalfield during the 1830s. Offenders against the code previously demanded by society members were secretly warned about their conduct and if they persisted were violently punished. An example of such a warning written in Welsh, and which had a long list of men's names written above, read

> *'TO ALL COLLIERS, TRAITORS, TURNCOATS AND OTHERS*
>
> *We hereby warn you the second and last time that we are determined to draw the hearts out of all the men above named and fix two hearts on the horns of the bull so that everyone may see what is the fate of every traitor and we know them all. So we testify with our blood.'*

Each branch or herd of the Scotch Cattle had its leader or *'bull'* chosen for his great strength and ferocious nature. He wore the skin and horns of a bull and carried a horn to warn of his approach. Other members of the herd, armed with cudgels, blackened their faces to avoid recognition. Some were dressed as women, others as children. The object of the raids was not only to terrify and punish the offenders but also to warn them about future conduct and to frighten others who might be tempted to disobey or to inform on local members of the gang. The herd broke up everything it could and heaped debris in the middle of a room and, in extreme cases, set it alight. The inhabitants of the cottages attacked were terrified and verbally abused, but their food and its containers were usually left intact. The herds did not gain universal approval and in some local Calvinistic churches members were urged to leave their herd and not to admit known Scotch Cattle members into their churches. The Oddfellows behaved similarly. Some of the activities ascribed to Scotch Cattle, as described in newspapers of the day, beggar belief. The following extracts are taken from the Monmouthshire Merlin

> **27 July 1834**: *'On Saturday morning last, at half past 12 o'clock, about 40 or 50 armed men, calling themselves Scotch Cattle, with faces blackened and handkerchieves round their heads, assembled in front of the house of Mr. Thomas Rees, at the Rock, in the parish of Bedwellty. They used tram plates as battering rams, forcing in the panels of the shop door, and with castings called chairs, in which the tram plates fit, demolished the upstairs windows, they entered the shop and stole a cask of butter, several cheeses, bacon, tobacco and every other article they could conveniently remove. They then tore the pages out of the shop books, and flung them into the road. Mr. and Mrs. Rees were so alarmed that they retreated to*

the back room and concealed themselves under a bed. These misguided men, from the experience they have had, are now able to enter any premises and sack the shop in 5 minutes. It would seem that the head and front of Mr. Rees's offending was, expressing his opinion on the impropriety of men leaguing against their employers. A short time back, a woman who resides near the Rock, secured her home, as she thought, and left, having occasion to go a few miles, and on her return she found the door forced, the windows broken, and nearly all she possessed two hours before taken away - in fact no person can travel from Risca to Tredegar without shuddering at the works of violence and wanton devastation that presents itself to the eye. (At this time the trains ran through Blackwood High Street. The line was not moved behind the High Street until 1865.)

1 Nov 1834: 'At 1 am on Tuesday last a number of men commenced a furious attack upon the Waterloo Shop, the property of Mr. W. Jones, in the parish of Bedwellty. Everything was destroyed.'

8 Nov 1834: 'On the night of Tuesday last at Blackwood, a poor woman named Joan Thomas received a gunshot wound in her arm, during an attack upon her house by those despicable miscreants called Scotch Cattle, from the effects of which she has since died. Vigilant efforts, we trust, are being made to discover the author of this dreadful event.'

7 Jan 1835: 'On Monday night (5 Jan) a party of those desperadoes called Scotch Cattle, broke into the house of Mr. Thomas Rees, shopkeeper, (described elsewhere as a coal merchant) near the Rock, Bedwellty, although the doors of the premises had been strongly barricaded and other precautions had been taken against them. The attack was commenced by the discharge of a musket, which so intimidated those within Mr. Rees's and the neighbouring houses, that not the slightest opposition was effected. The malefactors then commenced the wanton work of destruction, every article of furniture was broken into atoms, they forced open and carried away a massive iron chest, which contained, as is supposed, a large sum of money, and £40 belonging to an inmate, which had lately been left by a relation; 1 gold and 2 silver watches, and appendages, together with other property. They then attempted to set fire to the room in which Mr. and Mrs. Rees were, by placing burning curtains under their bed! Most providentially however in this the monsters failed, or the consequence would have been horrific in the extreme. Had the house taken fire, the explosion of several barrels of gunpowder that were on the premises would have destroyed the neighbourhood. We have heard that some men are now in custody, against whom strong suspicion exists of being concerned with this diabolical outrage. Surely it is high time that the authorities should adopt some strong measures to prevent a recurrence of such barbarities.'

In the late 1830s a local author wrote an account entitled *'The last 30 years in a Mining District'*. An extract relating to Scotch Cattle reads:

'The deeds of these barbarians were marked by one strange anomaly, the origin of which I never heard. If they entered a house, it was not to pillage, but to terrify its inmates, and before leaving they broke every single article of furniture; none was left unbroken, even to the fire-irons; but if there happened to be bread on the table, the table and bread were left untouched. It was considered sacrilege, and scrupulously to be avoided, the touching either of food (no matter what straits the intruders were reduced to), or the furniture on which it rested, or the cupboard in which it was placed.'

17 Jan 1835: *'Committed to Monmouth gaol on 8 Jan (what speed 'justice' then!) by Samuel Homphrey (Tredegar) and Edmund Williams (Maesruddud - Williams owned collieries and levels in Argoed and Hollybush): John James, otherwise Shoni Coal Tar, aged 33 and John Griffiths, aged 19, charged with having on Monday last broken into the dwelling house of Thomas Rees and stolen 136 sovereigns, promissory notes to the value of £70, £20 in silver, the property of Rees. On 12th William Jenkins, aged 31, also accused.'*

The assize court report on 4 April 1835 shows that John James and William Jenkins (who was a Welsh speaking baptist) were condemned to death but were later reprieved. The other two, John Griffiths and Thomas Jarman were found Not Guilty. At the same assize Edward Morgan, aged 32, was found guilty of the wilful murder of Joan Thomas at Bedwellty and was condemned to death. She had died as the result of an attack on 8 November last. John James and William Jenkins were sentenced instead to transportation for life. While imprisoned awaiting transportation William Jenkins made an unsuccessful attempt to escape. Shirts were torn into strips from which ropes were made.

9 Jan 1836: The editorial shows that local magistrates have the power to transport convicted persons for up to 14 years for minor offences such as *'nabbing a shoe or loaf of bread.'* This kind of offence is considered at the end of the day when perhaps only one magistrate is present apart from the Chairman. An urchin might be transported but the pawn-broker who receives the stolen article, and who may have put the boy up to it, gets paid for identifying the article.

On **5 March 1836** the newspaper reported that Edward Williams who was charged with leaving the service of his master Mr. James Treasure, of the parish of Bedwellty, was to be imprisoned for 3 months. Compare the relative power of the employer with the total helplessness of the employee. He could not even withdraw his labour without suffering heavy penalties.

2 May 1836: *'The house of Edward Rees near Blackwood had been burglariously entered and a cheque for £12, on the Banking House of Jones and Davies of Abergavenny, stolen therefrom; payment was stopped at the bank in Newport and Abergavenny. The cheque was presented at the bank of Messrs. Jones and Blewitt on Tuesday morning, and the chief cashier having heard of the circumstances, advised the person, (a respectable man, who had been requested to get the cheque cashed by a fellow in Bristol,* *and who was to call for the money), to bring Redman (the police officer) with him to Bristol, for the purpose of capturing the party who gave the cheque; this was done and when the packet (ship) arrived at Bristol at 11 o'clock in the morning, the man came on board: Capt. Young desired him to go to the cabin, but catching a glimpse of the officer (Redman) the fellow appeared as if affected by a coup de soleil (sun stroke), and perhaps for the benefit of his vision, he ran most rapidly, from the neighbourhood of the steam packets, but Redman apprehending something serious, started off after him to perform an operation, and felt his pulse in a garden, over the wall of which the patient had lept, impelled by the natural fear of the scalpel; he was now however taken care of, and couched (put to bed), and is now a valetudinarian (a person who is chronically sick) at the house of recovery at Usk, where his eyes will be opened to the serious state of his case. The fellow, as is supposed, by an optical delusion, found his way at night to the house of his old master, Edward Rees, where the watchdogs knew him; a carving knife and hatchet were found on the bed of the old people in the morning. Rees who formerly employed the prisoner is 87 years of age and his wife 83.'*

Mining jobs were insecure and miners often changed jobs several times a year - sometimes they worked only eight or nine months in a year. However, some miners were totally dedicated to improving their lot and, with help from John Moggridge, built their own houses and enclosed a small garden to grow their own vegetables. On the other hand most, even in good times, spent everything on food, drink, rent and furniture. In these poor economic circumstances, argued magistrate Edmund Williams of Maesrhuddud, indebtedness was a necessary evil. Almost everyone in Blackwood knew what it was like to beg or borrow. Men in debt found it hard to strike. Desperate conditions led to desperate measures. In 1832 between 250 and 300 Scotch Cattle men posted notices in the Blackwood area and proceeded to knock in the windows of 100 homes. The working class of Blackwood (and other nearby areas) were not only *'rebellious and easily roused'*, but were also past masters in the art of organisation, intimidation, and violence. It seems strange, but all they wanted to do was wreck everything. They did not want to take over the pits but they wanted to prevent the owners from creating wealth. By acting as they did they were removing the only way by which they - the workers - could earn the money to keep body and soul together. Perhaps their actions show how desperate they were.

The area was controlled politically by the Somersets and the Morgans of Tredegar. Efforts for independence were made by the Whig industrialist John Moggridge, Newport town-clerk and lawyer Thomas Prothero and John Frost, tailor and draper. The Whigs were originally a political party that opposed the succession to the throne of James, Duke of York because he was a catholic. They represented the great aristocracy and moneyed middle class. In the 18th and 19th centuries they had evolved so that they represented the desires of industrialists and Dissenters for political and social reform. They were the forerunners of the Liberals.

In 1832 only 4500 people in Monmouthshire could vote and by 1851 this area of Monmouthshire still had the lowest proportion of electors in the country. The Rock Inn was one of only eight places in the county where men could vote. When the Reform Bill was passed in 1832 there were celebratory athletics and fireworks displays in Blackwood. The number who could vote increased nationwide by about half-a-million but this did not satisfy for long. Prominent men in the area at this time included Samuel Etheridge (originally from Newport) and Thomas Havard (Blackwood). The Middle classes were pressurised to attend meetings but, complained Jacob Thomas, a shopkeeper from Maesycwmmer *'I am incessantly applied to by the Chartists, to assist them'*. Sarah Edmunds of the Greyhound, Pontllanfraith said *'We were not Chartists, but we were afraid to say no to the colliers.'* On one cold day in 1839, at Blackwood, Chartist missionaries from Pontypool and Newport, addressed several hundred colliers in the open air. On another occasion, at the Greyhound Inn, Edward Thomas spoke on the Charter for an hour and William Edwards followed with another long lecture. On yet another occasion Henry Vincent spoke to hundreds of colliers at the Greyhound. After tea, proceeded by a hundred flag-waving girls, Vincent travelled to the Coach and Horses, Blackwood where, in front of the hotel he participated in a large meeting chaired by Jack Barrill, one of the local secretaries. Most present, including many women and a few tradesmen, signed the

1. *The Greyhound Hotel when it still had tie-ups for horses along its frontage. It was the local meeting place for members of the Royal Ancient Order of Buffaloes and sold local ales and stouts brewed by Phillips and Sons.*

petition. Some returned to the Greyhound for an evening of penillion singing. After breakfast the following day William Davies, the radical son of a local shopkeeper, took Vincent, Edwards and three female Chartists to Gelligroes, where, in a large barn, Vincent was informed that scores of local colliers were joining associations and signing petitions. *'The labouring classes of Monmouthshire'* wrote one Blackwood collier *'have their eyes open and know from what quarter they are oppressed.'* By mid 1838 within two miles of Blackwood, lodges had appeared in nine places including Argoed, Croespenmaen, Gelligroes and Fleur-de-lys. At this time there were 32 collieries or levels within 2½ miles of the centre of Blackwood. In the 1830s a national movement known as Chartism expanded rapidly and in this area the Scotch Cattle seem to have evolved into Chartism. What did the Chartists want? They wanted six things -

2. *A later photograph of the Greyhound Hotel showing the depth of the three-storey building and the area in front which was suitable for large scale gatherings.*

Universal Suffrage, The Ballot, Annual Parliaments, Payment of MPs, Equal Electoral Districts and the Abolition of Property Qualifications. In 1839 conservative Methodist ministers and elders at Blackwood, stated that the Chartists were no more than *'infidels'* (unbelievers) and *'levellers'* (those advocating republicanism and freedom of worship). They refused to join the Chartists on the night of 3 Nov 1839. In an attempt to make life more bearable and to help one another when they were thrown out of work or suffered an accident a number of Friendly Societies had been set up, for example the Oddfellows and Welsh Ivorites. Many of these, though with good intentions, were not financially sound, so couldn't help as much as they had hoped when called upon to do so.

Henry Vincent, a Chartist lecturer, while on a visit to Blackwood in March 1839 stated that *'Miners are said to have good wages, but I have found this far from being the case. Work is very irregular. Some workmen, who joined the Chartist march had, at one time or another, been "absolutely without food"'*. Speaking after the November rising Esther Pugh of the Coach and Horses recalled *'About 8 or 9 months ago a lodge was opened at the large club room in the house which will hold about 60 people. There were a few shoemakers who began it first - one was Owen Davies. They were strangers to me. They said their object was to collect a few pence to buy some papers. The idea was that everybody had the chance to read these papers and so would know what was happening politically. By degrees people joined. The colliers of the neighbourhood were the principal ones.'* Members included Samuel Roberts, Richard Rorke and Thomas Llewellyn. William Barwell was secretary and Richard Pugh treasurer. At Pontllanfraith, under Jack Barrill, there was a male and a female Chartist society. Quite naturally political problems caused family arguments: Mary Ferriday, whose husband was killed alongside Abraham Thomas at Newport on that fateful November day, said *'I used to quarrel*

3. *The Coach and Horses, Blackwood, with its bricked-up window to reduce window tax. This was the meeting place for Chartists in the 1830s.*

on Mondays, with my husband about his going to the Chartist clubs at the Coach and Horses at Blackwood.' She admitted that other women used to mob and abuse her because she would not join.

At Blackwood, miners who refused to sign a Chartist petition and take a card could not expect to win or keep a job. Publicans and shopkeepers like Sarah Edmunds and Jacob Thomas gave regular assistance to the Chartists, but William Edmunds, a blacksmith and preacher from Argoed, refused to join a lodge and he was warned that he should seek *'the proper way of enlightenment'*. In April 1839 William Edwards claimed that he had 5000 followers at Blackwood who could be called together at the sound of a horn - a clear reference to the ways of Scotch Cattle. At Blackwood on Whit Monday 20 May 1839 there was a large gathering. The Monmouthshire Merlin estimated 4000 - 5000 but some newspapers claimed that there were many more. They came from Dowlais, Merthyr, Pontypool and Newport. The two principal speakers were William Jones and John Frost. The crucial decisions about the rising were put to a delegate meeting, held at the Coach and Horses on Friday, 1 November, 1839. There were 25-30 present and amongst those there were delegates from Dowlais, Dukestown, Rhymney, Sirhowy, Ebbw Vale, Blaina, Brynmawr, Llanelly Hill, Llanhilleth, Crumlin, Croespenmaen, Pontypool and Newport. Can you imagine why people from so wide an area would gather at Blackwood? It was the centre of militant Chartism in those days. The meeting was chaired by John Reynolds *'the preacher'* and coalhaulier. Frost spent the night at the Blackwood home of Job Tovey (originally from Bradford). At William Williams's beerhouse at Argoed on Saturday some 50 men were collected together under the watchful eye of two stewards and the 11 new members were called by name and told to obey a collier named Harry. As each contributed his 5d, his name was entered in a book. They were told to meet near the chapel (Baptist) early on Sunday morning, when their captain would give them instructions for later in the day. Those people in the neighbourhood who had not joined the association by that time would be the first to have their blood spilt.

Many workmen who wanted nothing to do with the Chartists, together with employers, managers, clerks, bankers, farmers, ministers of religion, shopkeepers and even constables, fled the area to such places as Abergavenny, Brecon and Crickhowell. The South Wales Daily News reported that *'respectable folk kept their horses saddled at night and hanged up hats, overcoats, bonnets and shawls near their head beds ready for immediate flight'*. They were afraid of the cry *'The Chartists are coming.'* One delegate to the meeting at the Coach and Horses, Thomas Giles told his colliers at The Colliers Arms (Gwrhay, Oakdale)

> *'Well boys, we are here everyone now in this house, you must attend to what I tell you seriously - every man that is now here is bound to be at Newport and go down with me tonight - every man that will turnback on his journey will be a dead man before 12 o'clock tomorrow and any man that stops in his house will be one and all dead men before 12 tomorrow - all the pits shall be broken to pieces and closed on the people in the levels - and every man must plunder every house as we go along and search for guns'.*

Imagine living here under those conditions. At Argoed it was reported that *'Husbands and sons were dragged from under beds and ordered forward at gunpoint'*. A few had been marked men. John Walters who kept the Castle Inn, Argoed, opposed the Chartists. When 20 men arrived at 6p.m. he and his sons refused to answer the call. A large rock was then rammed against the door, sending the bolt and locks flying through the room. *'Walters, you must come out'*, shouted one of the Chartists, *'your life is no better than ours.'* One of them put a gun to his chest and George Beach, sword in hand, handed Walters a shilling, and told him that he would not want for anything. In answer to the inevitable question, about their destination, Walters learnt that all would be revealed at Newbridge. In the Blackwood area there were many Chartists, Job Tovey being the most important. Others prominent in the area were the Batten and Fisher families of Gelligroes, Thomas Llewellyn and Benjamin Davies of Fleur-de-lys and William Ferriday, who died at Newport. He lived opposite the Lamb and Flag in Blackwood. Every ten men would be under a *'captain'*. The rising cry was *'Roll up! Roll up!'* and the password on the road was *'Beans'*. Answer *'Well'* and you were a Chartist. If not, your life was in danger for *'he was no friend of theirs, and they might do what they liked with him.'* The Blackwood contingent walked to Newbridge and then, via Abercarn, to the Royal Oak at Bassaleg. The weather was terrible. In the heavy rain they got soaked. The other groups failed to arrive as arranged, and the men got next to no sleep. Remember that they had left their homes in this valley on Sunday morning but did not get to the Westgate in Newport until Monday.

On the morning of Monday 4 Nov 1839 Thomas Phillips, the mayor of Newport, together with Captain Stack of the 45th regiment, was at the Westgate Hotel. Phillips had a copy of the Riot Act in his pocket. He sent to the nearby military barracks for help. Lt. Gray, Sergeants Daily and Armstrong and 28 privates (mainly young Irishmen under 23) arrived and stood guard in front of the hotel. Phillips then decided to put them in the yard behind the hotel but as the noisy mob came nearer they were called inside and put in a large end room in the east wing. From here they had a good view of the outside of the hotel. Also inside were at least 60 special constables. The Chartists entered the Westgate and shots were fired in the lobby. Who fired the first shot is still in doubt. It could even have been an accident. The special constables fled for their lives. Shots were fired by the Chartists in the direction of the specials. As a result some Chartists were hit by their own fire. In the space of about 15-20 minutes 22 chartists died. More than 600 pikes and guns were left in front of the Westgate by the fleeing Chartists. On this morning in November 1839 the British authorities inflicted greater casualties on the civilian population than at any other time in the 19th and 20th centuries.

After the events and court cases, leading local Chartists like William Davies and Job Tovey of Blackwood left their homes rather than face those protestors that returned. They had given evidence for the prosecution and so helped to convict the Chartist leaders. The marchers had been assured that the soldiers, or at least most of them, were really Chartist supporters and would not fire on them. They had been miserably misled. Thursday, 16th January 1840 was the day for the sentences. The law was much swifter then than it is today. John Frost, Zephaniah Williams and William Jones were condemned to the fate of traitors - death. The executions were fixed for Thursday 6th February. An executioner arrived in Monmouth and the scaffold was made ready. Many throughout the country sympathised with the Chartist cause. They were against the executions and widespread action was promised on the day. One comment in a radical newspaper read 'no Crown in Europe will be worth a year's purchase.' Violent protest took place in Manchester, and there were conflicts with the law in several places including London, Sheffield and Bradford. Threatening letters were sent to those connected with the prosecution. The death of Frost would probably have ruined preparations for Queen Victoria's impending marriage to Albert and some believed that it might well bring down the Whig government - it did fall in 1841. Lord Granville Somerset, Octavius Morgan, and Samuel Homphray wanted the leaders to suffer the death penalty. How the Prime Minister (Viscount Melbourne) and his colleagues came to change their minds is a mystery. However, reasons were found to commute the death sentences to transportation. The three were immediately moved to Chepstow, 15 days later they were shipped to Plymouth, and within a week put on the convict ship *Mandarin* for their five months journey to Australia. William Jones died in Australia in December 1873 and Zephaniah Williams in Tasmania in 1874. The conditions that Zephaniah Williams endured during the remainder of his life are recorded in letters to his wife. They can only be described as atrocious. John Frost returned to England in 1856 and lived with his sister in Bristol until he died.

After the events of 1839 the authorities concluded that the Welsh had become as ungovernable as the Irish! Anglicization, it was believed, was the only possible cure. Almost every informed observer believed that the Chartists were within a hair's breadth of a dramatic victory, and the beginning of a possibly successful guerrilla war. The leaders, many believed, wanted to establish a Chartist Republic. Our area was a unique industrial society, where the process of change was faster and the impact more socially divisive than perhaps anywhere else in Britain. It was a class society from birth and the coexistence, in some districts, of a native workforce and an outside body of employers, shopkeepers, tradesmen, teachers, clergy and law officers helped to give its industrial relations a special character.

Little had changed at the top some 30 years later for the 1881 census shows that in Blackwood the vicar was from Glamorgan, the curate Carmarthen, the Governess from Bristol, the Station Master from Pembroke, the Farm Bailiffs from Mid Wales and Somerset, the colliery manager, watchmaker, newsagent, blacksmith, boot and shoemakers, and rail inspector from Gloucester or Somerset. The area could not produce its own entrepreneurs, professional or business men.

The main objectives of the Chartists seemed to be political rights and not to take over the means of production. Eventually all their requests were met except annual parliaments. Had Frost been executed it is quite possible that Britain would have experienced unprecedented popular violence. When you pass the site of the Coach and Horses at the bottom of town or take your pet to the vet in the former Greyhound Hotel spare a thought for what went on in and around those buildings 160 years ago. Those events might well have changed the history of our country and hence the world.

Following the events of 1839 the miners lost their militancy. Reform was slow to come and the employers remained as tough as ever. *'There is terrorism existing over the men'*, said Joseph Thomas, a blacksmith of Pontllanfraith in 1841 *'and they dare not speak out.'* Thomas was referring to employer control, namely *'long pay'*, (they were paid every 4 or 5 weeks) and the truck system. Coal still dominated the local economy in the 1950s. A report of that time shows that of the 5270 men employed in the Blackwood/Pontllanfraith

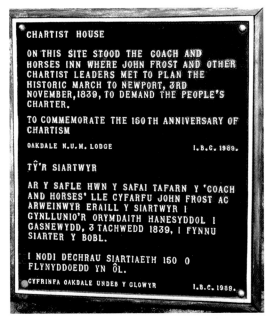

4. *The bi-lingual plaque indicating the site of the Coach and Horses on the west side of the High Street at the southern end of the down.*

area, 4057 earned their living in the collieries of Rock, Waterloo, Oakdale, Wyllie and Nine Mile Point. After almost 200 years coal has disappeared from our economy for ever. We must remember the trials and tribulations of our forebears which led to the objectives of the charter being attained.

CHAPTER 2

Blackwood Town

5. Blackwood High Street during the first decade of the 20th Century. It looks as though the block to the south of the old Post Office (now Currys) is in the process of construction. Building is also taking place on the opposite side of the road and just south of The George. Note the gas lamps on the west side of the street, the unmade road, the bunting and St. George's flag outside The George. What occasion did this celebrate? Was it the Coronation of King Edward VII?

6. The east side of the central part of Blackwood High Street one sunny morning c1905. Most of the buildings remain today except that the house between the Porters (then the Butchers Arms) and Going Places has yet to give way to what became known as the Dorothy Café. How low the ceilings were in that house.

7. London House on The Square, Blackwood as it was pre-1914. The business belonged to Lewis Jones and specialised in drapery, hosiery and millinery. While this building has been replaced by a similar one (Argos) the right hand side of the street is totally changed. That the horse was the means of moving goods is much in evidence!

13

8. A very early picture of Blackwood High Street looking south from present-day Woolworths. The road, with its gas lights, has yet to be tarmacadamed. The modes of transport are on foot, riding a bicycle or by horse. On the immediate right is the building occupied by present-day Tidals Stores. In the middle distance the Foresters Arms is on the right with the Butchers Arms a little further on. The building housing the ironmongers on the left has been replaced but the next substantial block still stands.

9. Blackwood High Street c1948. While the buildings on the eastern side of the street are more or less intact, all have changed uses. Hodges (Gents outfitters) has gone, so have Peglers (grocers), Cash & Co. (footwear), the Red & White bus offices, and the London Hosiery (Fashion and Drapery). On the western side of the street The Square Café is the only business still in existence. The Bargoed Radio and Cromwell Jones (grocers) have also disappeared while the iron railings and garden have given way to Woolworths.

10. Blackwood High Street looking north c1958. It shows buses at their stands on both sides of the High Street, a stand without a bus in front of the main Post Office (now Currys) and a terrace of houses on the site of present day Wilkinsons, next to the Maxime Cinema.

11. Blackwood High Street from outside the Foresters Public House in the mid 1950s. Batemans the grocer has been replaced by Fads, the alley to Blackwood Builders Supply now leads to Broomfield and Alexander (Accountants), Lamberts, which has consolidated further down the High Street, is now Shaws the drapers, Sumptions the Chemist and Optician has become Savers, Dewhurst the butcher is an Estate Agent and Boots the Chemist has moved twice - it is now on the opposite side of the road and part of the new shopping precinct.

12. Blackwood High Street looking north from a spot near the bottom of Gordon Road very early in the last century. The main building on the left, which belonged to A.E. Smith the newsagent, still stands but the row of white cottages beyond was replaced by the Post Office and Sorting Office. Note the gas lamp well out into the road, the open space opposite and the house set at right angles to the road.

13. A scene showing a businessman dealing with his customers in Lilian Road, Blackwood, between the wars. Lilian Road runs parallel to the High Street immediately behind the bus station.

14. The view from the Poundstretcher corner (then Leslie's Stores) c1940. It is interesting to see a bucket (for ashes - no wheelie bins then) on the edge of the pavement outside the Red and White offices and a Belisha beacon, indicating a place where pedestrians should cross, a little further along the street. There were no road markings in those days, simply a yellow sphere surmounting a black and white pole on each side of the road.

15. A gathering of children and young people outside the Foresters Public House in 1905. The boy with folded arms in the front is Sam Coleman, who was later to run the business of A. Coleman & Son, Fishmonger and Fruiterer, on Blackwood High Street. The pace of life was rather slower on the High Street then than it is today!

16. A 1930s gypsy caravan standing on the ground that is now part of Sunningdale Nurseries. The building behind the caravan housed machinery and belonged to the former Rock Colliery. On the other side of the railway embankment the Palace cinema can be seen in the centre. This ceased to function as a cinema soon after the outbreak of the 1939-45 war. Subsequently it became Babers main showroom but is now Wetherspoons.

17. The southern end of Blackwood town from Woodfieldside in 1948. The steep hill near the centre is Gordon Road which leads from the High Street to Plas Farm, now The Monkey Tree. The photograph shows how the need for housing after WW II was satisfied by providing prefabricated bungalows. Those shown were erected on what became known locally as 'New Albany'. The houses were much loved by most people who lived in them and lasted far longer than the twenty years it was estimated they would be good for.

18. This photograph shows Oakdale Terrace, Penmain, which is part of the main road from Blackwood to Oakdale. The northern part of Blackwood can be seen in the distance. The prominent road on the right hand side leads from the main road to Maesrhuddud. It was laid to make the journey easier for horse drawn vehicles but is no longer used. To the left of this road is the Gelli Farm and in the centre we can just make out the colliery buildings which stood on the present day Lon Pennant.

19. Pontllanfraith with Blackwood in the distance. In the very centre of the picture is the Plough Corner with Newbridge Road stretching out to the right. The Springfield estate is yet to be built on the fields in the foreground.

20. A 1915 view of Oakdale colliery and village from the top of the foundry hill, Blackwood. The wall in the foreground, as seen from the road and railway below, is the best example of a dressed stone retaining wall in the area.

CHAPTER 3

The Surrounding Villages

21. King Street, Cwmfelinfach, known locally as The West End, in 1905. This street is parallel to the main road through the village (Maindee Road) on its western side. The corner shop on the right was Addinbrooks, where you could buy almost anything. If a teacher sent you there with 3d to buy a cane you could be sure it would be used on you first!

22. Maindee Road, Cwmfelinfach, in 1918. Hughes (draper) and Price (Post Office, but also a draper) were on the left. French (another draper), Johnson & Johnson and Silverthorns on the right. While the road looks satisfactory in the foreground, it is non existent in the middle distance. The main road down the valley was behind the houses on the right. On the right a mother carries her child wrapped in a shawl in a manner often referred to as 'Welsh' fashion.

23. A very early photograph of Cwmfelinfach often referred to years long ago as Cwmfelinfach Ynysddu. This was probably a consequence of Ynysddu being older than Cwmfelinfach.

24. The Dingle, Cwmfelinfach, in 1960. This picturesque dell is found by turning north off Twyn-Gwyn Road. A walk along here will eventually lead to the disused Nant y Draenog reservoir. Years ago the stream in this dingle would be dammed when a baptismal pool was required to initiate new members into the local Baptist Church.

25. The centre of Ynysddu in 1905 looking west with the railway line down the valley in the distance. This picture was taken long before the wide main road down the valley which was built beyond the properties in the foreground. The new road was obviously too straight and wide for modern traffic as numerous speed reduction measures were introduced in the year 2000. The road in the mid-distance leads under the railway bridge to the station. The property on the left belonged to John Hughes, greengrocer.

26. Glen View, Ynysddu, c1920. The message on this postcard is amusing. It reads: Dear Myfanwy. My loving pet. I'm still alive. I'm not dead yet. Grannie.

27. Commercial Street, Ynysddu, c1930. Now relatively quiet this street used to carry all the traffic that travelled up and down the valley.

28. Ynysddu Railway Station c1912. Two well-dressed gentlemen with 'boaters', closely followed by their ladies, stand on the platform awaiting a train. There are two large wicker baskets, called skips (What would they have been used for?) and a wooden wheelbarrow on the platform. Behind is the village, including three-storey houses on the left.

29. A mid-century view of Wyllie village as seen from the east. The colliery stands to the left and the Methodist Church is in the centre. Both have long since gone.

30. Nant y Draenog reservoir on the eastern mountainside above Cwmfelinfach. It belonged to Abertillery & District Water Board and was the end of the supply line from the Grwyne Fawr reservoir. From here it supplied the valley to the south until 1972. The properties on the far shore were taken down, due to sewage problems, soon after the reservoir became operational. In the 1960s, consequent upon a clean Sirhowy river after the closure of the collieries, several fishing clubs thrived in the area. However, these fishermen soon decided that they needed still water. While Penyfan Pond satisfied one club, two clubs were in dispute over Nant y Draenog. As the dispute could not be settled amicably by Mynyddislwyn (later Islwyn) Council the matter was passed to a County Council Commission. In due course they decided to close it and release the dammed water because no toilets were available there for the fishermen!

31. The view of Pontllanfraith looking north-east from Pontllanfraith Great Western Railway Station, that is the lower station. This photograph, taken early in the century, shows the schools on the left. These substantial buildings are still in use today.

32. Old Penllwyn, former home of a member of the Morgan family, looking a sorry sight in 1905.

33. Gelligroes village c1948. Taken from the old road to Ynysddu looking towards the Penllwyn. The building in the centre is the famous old mill which today is open to the public as a museum. In the distance are the bungalows along Blackwood Road and the conspicuous flat-roofed house belonging at that time to the Camm family.

34. Looking towards Pontllanfraith and the Penllwyn from the east in 1960. The terrace in the foreground is Sir Ivor's Road; in the centre are the Mynyddislwyn Council Offices and the Catholic Church. Pontllanfraith Grammar School is on the right and a partly built Penllwyn stands on the hill behind.

35. Gelligroes village from the north c1948. The signal box controlled the three lines coming together here. The road on the right, next to the signal box, was the main road down the valley. It passed between the houses (Heolddu Road), crossed the river at Gelligroes Mill and can be seen ascending the hill leading to Ynysddu on the left of the picture.

36. Maesrhuddud House, a Tudor style mansion one mile north of Blackwood, was built for Edmund Williams the colliery owner at the beginning of the twentieth century. It is L-shaped and was built in two stages. Stage 1, the north-east wing, was designed by E.P. Warren and erected in 1900. Stage 2 followed in 1907 when the original farm house was replaced by the south-west wing. The next owner, Brewer Williams, had a grander vision. He employed Thomas Mawson to lay out a stately garden with the intention of building a much larger and more expensive looking house. Warren drew up plans for a larger house in 1914 but the only part of the design that came to fruition was the coach-house. Inside the house are two beautiful chimney pieces and much impressive wood-work. After Brewer Williams's day the property was used by various organisations, eventually becoming on Old People's Home run by the council until it was sold and converted to the Maes Manor Hotel. Significant alterations and additions have taken place in recent years including the roofing over of the courtyard to become an attractive function room. Today Maes Manor is a very pleasant place to spend a few hours.

37. The Rock Inn, Blackwood, one of the oldest buildings in the area still in regular use. It is shown here sandwiched between two cottages which it has since absorbed. The tracks suggest that the hill to Maesrhuddud was used as much as the main road. In the 18th Century the Rock Inn was one of only eight places in the county of Monmouthshire where voters could register their vote at election time. Magistrates, such as John Moggridge, the founder of Blackwood, also conducted hearings and administered justice from this building.

38. Looking north along Bedwellty Road, Cefn Fforest c1922. To the right is the Twynyffald office of the London Joint City and Midland Bank. This property subsequently became Cefn Fforest Police Station. In the middle distance three children play quite happily and safely on the edge of the pavement. No traffic problems then.

39. Looking south along Penybryn Avenue, Cefn Fforest, with the school on the right, c1920. The school was opened in 1915 and by July 1916 had 9 teachers and 369 pupils. It says much about the times to read in the school log that in September 1916 several pupils 'sat for labour'. This was a very basic examination which enabled pupils who passed to leave school earlier than usual provided they had a job to go to. Many of these were as young as 11 years of age. Compared with those days we have little to complain about.

40. The shops opposite the school in Cefn Fforest in the 1950s. Bill Granville unloads goods from his large Vauxhall saloon. A Ford Anglia with a cutback rear window stands outside the Co-operative store.

41. Oakdale Terrace, Penmain, the main road linking Oakdale with Blackwood, c1910. The message on this postcard relates that a woman had recently burned to death in one of the houses at the top of the picture.

42. Syr Dafydd Avenue, Oakdale, one pleasant summer's day in the 1920s. E.H. Chivers, a name on many an old postcard of the area, owns the Post Office which was in the same building as it is today. They sell Blue Bell tobacco and Fry's chocolate. The shop further away belongs to Thomas & James. They sell Lyons tea as well as those popular brands of cigarettes Woodbine and Players Please. Nearer the camera, outside the shop of W. Thomas & Son, a man in a grocer's apron (Mr. Thomas?) stands next to a van. The adjacent shop belonging to A. Morgan, advertises Exide batteries and has a scrubbing board for sale outside. This block has two oriel upstairs windows. The trees along the avenue are relatively young.

43. The Square, Oakdale, c1950, with the War Memorial in the centre in the form of a cross. This has since been replaced. At that time the thriving shops looked out on well kept lawns and flower beds. Oakdale is an impressive horseshow village; a product of the Garden City movement of the early twentieth century, one of several planned housing schemes in Wales that arose directly from the Housing Act of 1909. The village was built between 1909 and 1924 for miners at the local colliery and is set out on level ground above the colliery. The relatively spacious layout of the streets and public places is in stark contrast to the cramped and tightly packed terraced housing of mining communities in the previous century.

44. St. David's Avenue, Oakdale, c1916. The houses, being new, are in pristine condition. Two schoolboys look extremely well dressed with their straw hats and white collars; the pavements have been laid, young trees have taken root but it will be some years before the tarmacadam arrives for the road.

45. This photograph was taken almost a century ago from a point just north of the New Inn, Bedwellty. It shows buildings that were standing a long time before that. The most distant house (now called Homelands) was marked The Cottage on the Tithe map of 1839 and Church Cottage on later maps. Early on, it was owned by the wealthy Fothergill family and in 1871 was occupied by Thomas Ellis, the famous mining engineer who was colliery manager at Tredegar. By 1881 Church Cottage was occupied by Isaiah Thomas, a miners' agent with nine children. Originally a stone property it was encased in bricks (and rendered) in the twentieth century.

The buildings on the right consist of a schoolroom - note the large window at the far end of the block - and three cottages. The schoolroom has Victorian features but there had been a school here or in the vicinity before Victoria came to the throne for it is on record that in 1768 there was a school on the highway near Bedwellty church - 'Henry Morgan of Caerleon, acquired from Isaac Lewis, Bedwellty, a cottage to be kept and used for instructing children and inhabitants of Bedwellty in the Protestant Religion'. The head was to be appointed by Henry Morgan and his heirs. The school we can just make out in the photograph closed around the time of World War I and was later used as a Sunday School for the nearby parish church. In 1841 John Evans, the schoolmaster, lived in the cottage next to the school while by 1881 the second cottage is recorded as being a mineral water or pop factory. Bottles have been found bearing the name Phillips, Bedwellty which help to support this fact. The end cottage housed the blacksmith; ten people lived in this small cottage including the blacksmith's striker. Close inspection shows that the lean-to building nearest the camera had an arched entrance which was subsequently blocked up but with the inclusion of a door and a window. This was probably the smithy since it is high enough and wide enough for a horse to enter. In 1881 the census records that eight people lived in the New Inn (just the middle section of the present day pub) and eleven in Church Cottage.

The 1839 Tithe Map shows that the land in this picture was part of the Tredegar Estate belonging to Sir Charles Morgan. The field names are interesting: the field immediately opposite the terrace is Cae'r Pentre - the village field - and the field visible in the picture Waun y Pentre - the village meadow. It is probable that many village activities took place here. Since WW II three fields have become graveyards. They are Cae Pen Heol - the field at the top of the road (the graveyard nearest Cefn Fforest); Cae'r Gongl - the corner field - and Erw'r Gangell - the chancel acre. The 1881 Census gives the population of the village as 68 which is somewhat more than at present!

46. Abernant Road, Markham in the early 1940s. Jones & Porter the grocers and the Sub-Post Office are two of the businesses that face the colliery on the other side of the valley.

47. Markham Terrace, Markham village c1930. The village and colliery were named after Arthur Markham the company chairman. The white buildings in the distance belong to Berllanlwyd Farm. Following a serious fire many years ago the area was cleared. I am given to understand that there are now bungalows on the site which is adjacent to Markham Institute.

48. When the village of Markham was planned the provision of shops seems to have been forgotten. Villagers had to go to Argoed to do their shopping. This was inconvenient and undesirable and so in 1916 the block of three shops shown in the photograph was built on the main Blackwood - Tredegar road within easy reach of the village. Viewed from the right they were: the Post Office run by Mr. and Mrs. Powell, the grandparents of Sue Carpenter, the present postmistress of Markham; a grocery shop, which later became Mrs. Bora's wool and fancy goods shop, and the butchers' shop belonging to brothers John and Llewellyn Morgan. When the Post Office moved to the centre of the village and other shops opened in adjacent properties, the pressure became too much for the businesses left on the main road and they were soon forced to close. Near by, the Conservative Club stood as a wooden structure on stilts. The opportunity afforded by the closure of the shops was too good to miss. Chiefly as a result of the endeavours of Chairman Arthur Holley together with Bill Turner and Harry Webb, the building was taken over by the existing Conservative Club and altered so that it could be used as a club. Much of this conversion was carried out by George Jones later to found the builders' merchants business of Geo. W. Jones & Sons, Blackwood. When conversion was complete the club opened under its new name of Markham Social Club, but soon became known as The Bottom Club. It was a three-storey building with living accommodation for the steward and his family, and was Men Only. Subsequently a new Blue Room was added at the rear. Changes in the way people lived, not least the ease with which they could travel, resulted in the use of the club diminishing and ultimately closing. After lying idle for several years the dilapidated building was taken down in the late 1990s. Other points of interest in this photograph are the white building on the left which was the 'village hall', and the tram lines which cross the main road and run down the slope towards the spot where Markham baths would be built some years later. A gas lamp stands on the corner leading from Newport Road to Markham Terrace and Abernant Road. A mother and children are just visible in Pen y werlod Terrace on the extreme left.

In the distance, just above the hip line of the roof, we can see Great Western Cottages and the chapel in Hollybush, adjacent to which is Banalog Terrace. Various farms are scattered on the surrounding hillside. These include Uplands Farm and the farms of Penyrheol Fawr and Llwyn-arfon.

49. The Workmen's Library and Institute in Fleur-de-lys as it looked before the extension to each end and before the extra storey was added. The institute was built in 1911 at a cost of £1800. The completed building had a Dance Floor and Lending Library and in recent years the top floor was used for a Boxing Club under the watchful eye of former boxer Dai Gardener. Among the boxers who learnt their craft there was Johnny Owen the Merthyr Matchstick. A few years ago the upper storey was seriously damaged by fire. It has been repaired but is now a club with a licensed bar. St. David's Church is visible in the background.

50. A very early photograph of the High Street, Fleur-de-lys taken from a point near the junction of Ford Road with the High Street. The direction of the camera is towards Maesycwmmer. The Trelyn Arms is on the right and Salem Welsh Congregational Chapel almost opposite. This chapel was built in 1860 and demolished in 2000.

51. Commercial Street, Aberbargoed looking towards New Tredegar, as it appeared during World War I.

52. The Workmen's Library and Institute, Aberbargoed, showing Cwrt-Coch Street and Elm Street in the background c1910. This building is now a residential home.

53. The Powell Duffryn Hospital, Aberbargoed, in the 1930s. This hospital was opened in 1909. It could accommodate twenty-four patients and was supported by miners contributions.

Religion

54. Babell Chapel and Islwyn's monument, Cwmfelinfach.

55. William Thomas was the youngest of the three sons of Morgan and Mary Thomas, an English speaking couple living at Ynysddu. He was born at the Old Machine House (Ty'r Agent), on the third of April 1832. His father was employed as a mineral agent by Benjamin Hall (later Lord Llanover) of Big Ben fame. Morgan's two elder sons followed in their father's footsteps to become surveying and mining engineers but other thoughts evolved in the mind of William. His family were well-off, which accounts for the fact that he was educated at private schools in Tredegar and Newport before proceeding to Cowbridge Grammar School. From the grammar school William was sent to the Normal College at Swansea where he began his studies with the intention of becoming a mining engineer. At college he met Ann Bowen but sadly, she died prematurely in 1853. Her death was a traumatic event for William, something from which he never fully recovered. William soon decided that engineering was not for him. His thoughts moved to religion, he was taught Welsh by his brother-in-law and he was initiated into the mysteries of Welsh poetry by Aneurin Jones, a miller at nearby Gelligroes. Aneurin Jones known locally as Aneurin Fardd, apart from being a poet, was also a historian and author. He kept the Halfway Inn at Gelligroes, and was the life and soul of the village. However his talents did not extend as far as sound finance and when he became insolvent he fled to America leaving his debts behind him. There he became an important man living to a great age. He was finally laid to rest in Los Angeles. William's father, Morgan Thomas, had been instrumental in the building of Babell Calvinistic Methodist chapel in Cwmfelinfach. The chapel was built on the site of the former Babell Row, which had housed horse handlers for the local tramroad. Rev. William Thomas, who had worked as a newspaper editor in Newport before being called to the Calvinistic cause, was the minister in Babell until he died on 20 November 1878 at the age of 46. He is best known by his bardic title Islwyn. His nom-de-plume was taken from the nearby mountain, and was used when he submitted poems to eisteddfodau throughout Wales. He won many first prizes, but never the National. His most important work is Y Storm which he wrote in memory of his beloved Ann. At the time of his death, Islwyn lived at Y Glyn, opposite the old Post Office on the top road in Ynysddu. He is buried at Babell and the building now acts as a museum housing many items associated with him. When you enter the old chapel a wax effigy of this famous preacher and poet stands in the pulpit to greet you. He contributed much to the local community including writing many of the inscriptions to be found on gravestones at Abercarn cemetery.

56. A closer view of Islwyn's monument, Cwmfelinfach.

57. Sardis Church, Ynysddu, latterly the United Reform Church, shown here in 1909 when it was about to be completed, as were the houses in the background. The inscription on the front of the building in Welsh translates to Independents (Congregationalists) School Room.

58. The interior of Argoed Baptist Chapel, showing its horsebox pews of 1852. The centre of the pulpit can be removed to reveal a baptistry.

The extraction of coal started in and around Argoed in 1810, and attracted workers from many areas including baptists from Tredegar, Caerphilly, Hengoed and Blaina. It was not long before these workers set up a Baptist Community in the area, the home of William Meredith being licensed as a meeting room in 1811. The first baptism was performed by Pastor John Jenkins in the same year. Soon afterwards Mr. Yoreth, a kind and generous landowner gave permission for services to be held in his house. In 1816 a parcel of land was leased for 999 years from Mr. Yoreth for 1/- (5p) a year so that a church could be built with an adjacent graveyard. The deed was executed by a solicitor on behalf of the London Baptist Building Fund and the building was duly opened in 1817. The first preacher was Pastor Harry Harry the son of Pastor Evan Harry of Blaenau Gwent. Yoreth gave the stones that were needed for the chapel at an estimated cost of £60. At this time there were 37 members. When Yoreth died he left the land to his son who, almost immediately, decided that he wanted the adjacent land to build houses on. To prevent this the members leased additional land which resulted in the rent increasing to 20/- (£1) a year. In 1818 Pastor Thomas Davies of Ruabon, North Wales, accepted the call and settled in Argoed in July 1818. He was forty and came with a reputation of being a poetic genius, humorous and with a quick wit. The debt on the building, which started as £416, was cleared by 1834. A Bargoed branch was set up and Caersalem, Aberbargoed was established in 1839. By this time the membership at Argoed was 86 with 90 scholars attending Sunday School. They were taught by 11 teachers. In 1851 it was felt that the chapel was dilapidated and had become too small so a new building was erected and more land leased to extend the graveyard. The extra cost was less than £400 and the ground rent was increased to 30/- (£1.50) a year. The chapel reopened on 2 February 1852. In 1875 a house was built for the minister William Thomas of Beaufort at a cost of £300. He was pastor for more than a decade but in 1886 emigrated to Nova Scotia. It was 2½ years before there was a new pastor. Membership continued to increase: 139 in 1900 and 197 in 1909 when there were also 320 youngsters on the books of the Sunday School. Expansion continued with the establishment of a church in Hollybush. This opened on 20th November 1884.

59. The medieval church of St. Tudor's, Mynyddislwyn, from the north east as it looked c1910. The original church was rebuilt on a larger scale c1820. Only the west tower remained untouched. The tower, with its three string courses, has a north east stair-turret which rises high above its battlements. The picture shows two iron-clad windows in the north wall and the two Perpendicular windows at the east end which are attributed to E.M. Bruce in the restoration of 1907.

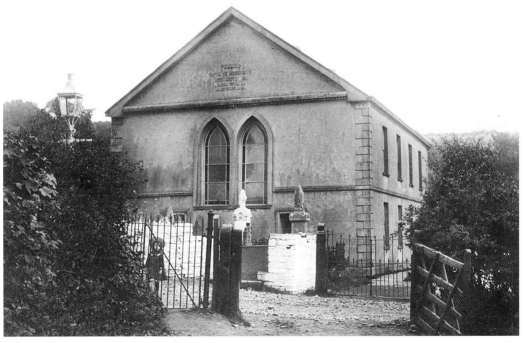

60. Penmain Independent Chapel during the first decade of the last century. Note the unmade road, the gas lamp on the left, the kissing gate and the stone stile into the chapel grounds. The building is now the practice room for Mynyddislwyn Male Voice Choir.

61. The interior of the Central Methodist Church, Blackwood during the last service before major alterations began in August 1988. The church was built by Rosser and Roberts of Abercarn in 1898 and was thought extremely modern for the times. According to John Newman in *The Buildings of Wales* the design is Gothic, faced with purple glazed brick. It has cuspless tracery and twin segment headed doorways of pale ashlar stone. There is a handsome ribbed segmental ceiling and stained glass in a typical repeating Art Nouveau pattern.

62. Jerusalem Independent Chapel in the winter snow of 1962-63. This was built by a break-away group from Penmain. It has now been re-roofed and converted into a two-storey private residence. Although the general impression of the frontage of the building is unchanged, the original tall chapel windows with rounded heads on the side wall have been blocked up and rectangular windows inserted. The building now looks extremely well cared for, which is a lot more than can be said for the graveyard!

63. Members of the Sunday School of the Central Methodist Church, Blackwood, passing Mount Pleasant Baptist Church during their Whitsun walk c1950. From the rear of the photograph the group includes Robert Dearth, Tim Davies, Andrew Davies; Jean Parsons, Dorothy Coggins, Sally Davies, Joyce Downing, Claire Prosser, Pauline Shore (carrying Sally Davies); Hilda Woodward, Alice Bennett, May Parsons, Mal Brown, D.M. Williams (organiser), Blanche Thomas, Alma Bennett, Gordon Bennett, Noreen Jones, A. Thomas, Anthony Burrows, David Jones, Peter Davies, Roger Lewis, Elizabeth Lewis, Margaret Evans, Victor Norman (waving); Percy Trigg, Gary Gane, David Onions, Jim Shore (carrying Michael) Len Brown, Derek Burrows, Albert Doughty, Murray Jones, Gordon Groves, Greg Groves, Clive Williams, Ivor James, Billy James, C.A.M. Bennett, Billy Davies, Rev E.R. Pickard, A. Mortimer, Harry Tucker.

64. Part of the congregation taken during the last service (August 1988) to be held at the Central Methodist Church, Blackwood, before it closed pending major internal alterations. The church was divided into two at the level of the gallery, the upstairs becoming the church and the ground floor a multi-purpose room. One sad factor of the redevelopment was the destruction of the organ (given by the Tucker family several decades previously) but it appears that much money was needed to be spent on it to bring it up to the necessary standard. Included in the group are: Jeff Mudford, Christine Howarth, Marilyn Angel, Valerie Edwards, Ruby Jardine, Jeffrey Ellis, Jean Evans, Joan (Edwards), Rev David Howarth, Olwen Button, Margaret Bleazard, Bill Bleazard, Pauline Waite, John Nicholas, Molly James, Betty Price, Hilary Price, Alma Bennett, Alice Bennett, Edna Gane, Blanche Thomas, Ethel Jones, Brenda Evans, Harold Price.

65. St. Sannan's Church, Bedwellty, from the south-west. Note the orientation of the gravestones. The graves are set east - west with the headstone at the west end. This is because people were laid in their graves facing the rising sun awaiting the resurrection. This practice is still observed today.

66. A view of the tower wall of St. Sannan's Church, Bedwellty, taken from the nave. A most unusual feature is a stone circle set within a stone circle high up in the wall and shown on the left of the picture. To my knowledge no similar feature appears in any church in the diocese and, despite much delving, no satisfactory explanation has been offered for its existence.

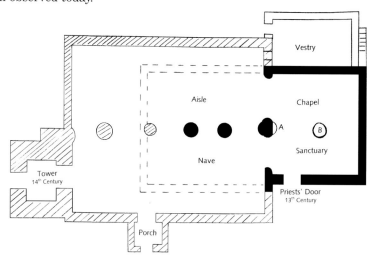

67. The solid line shows the walls of the 13th Century church that still remain; the hatched lines show walls that were added in the 14th Century. The broken lines show the supposed position of the 13th Century walls which were removed when the church was enlarged in the 14th Century. The unshaded area at A indicates where an early respond has been cut away to reveal several mason marks. B marks the probable position of an original pier. The vestry, with a cellar underneath which is now used as a boiler room, was added c1910. When its foundations were prepared it was necessary to exhume the remains of eighteen burials.

68. The inside of St. Sannan's Church c1910 before the installation of the organ.

St. Sannan's Church, Bedwellty. Extracts from the Churchwarden's Book (1780-1898)
For comparison with today's money 1 shilling i.e. 1s or 1/- is equal to 5p and 6d or 6 old pence equates to $2^{1}/2$p. Anything in brackets is my addition.

1780 Lime 11/-. For white liming of church 6/-, tyler £1.

1783 Ale at three Parish Meetings 3/-, To Gregory Perrot for 1300 tyles 15/-, digging a sawpit 1/6, slitting 4000 lathes 10/-.

1788 1/- for Prayer for King's Recovery.

1795 6 bottles wine 16/7, manchet (the finest wheaten bread) 6d.

1799 Paid 10/6 reward for killing a fox and 1/- reward for killing a badger.

29 Oct 1813 Assessment for repairs, etc. for the church, rate of 6d in the pound. (Properties were given a valuation on which a rate was charged to support the Parish Church. For example the valuation of Gellydwyll Farm, on the left of the main road as you leave Blackwood for Tredegar, was £3.10s. A rate of 6d in the £ meant that the taxes due to the church on this property were 20d for the year, that is, about 8p. The Churchwardens at the time were Rosser Thomas and Charles Ellis while the valuations were signed by Richard Fothergill JP and Matthew Monkhouse JP, all four of whom were important businessmen/property owners in the area.)

1815 Repair stible (steeple or tower) £32.

1817 Paid Edmund Miles on account for making Pews £9.8.4$^{1}/2$. (These were probably the pews that were in the church until the restoration at the turn of the century. Some of them were removed to the Mill at Gelligroes and the timber from them can still be seen there.) Paid Thomas Thomas for paving church £3.10. Sexton (grave digger) 2-year's wages 6/-.

9 July 1819 To hair to put in mortar 1/- . (This was horsehair to mix with the mortar with which they torched the roof, i.e. they filled the cracks between the stone tiles to stop the wind and rain driving in. This was before the days of felt and was most effective if done properly.)

Sept. 1820 To Howell Howells for halling (hauling) stones from Rumney river to Bedwellty Church 12/-
(By 1841 the total assessment or valuation for the area was up to £3595 and £150, at a rate of 10d in the £ was collected for church funds. The Public Houses mentioned on or near Blackwood High Street were the Royal Oak and the George. The beerhouses were Red Lion, Crown, Yew Tree, Lamb and Flag, Coach and Horses, New Royal Oak, Butchers Arms and Masons Arms. At this time the Rhymney Company objected to paying the rates. They claim that by Act of Parliament they are exempt because they have a district church of their own.)

1848 Coalbrook Dale Co. for church stove £14, carriage £1, copper pipe £7.2s. (There were many references after this to the buying of coal. The sexton receives a salary of £2 p.a. and in addition is paid £2 p.a. for cleaning the church.)

1857 Collecting money for the church by a rate of every property is abandoned. From now on the costs are to be met by voluntary contributions.

1893 From now on collections taken at services.

1894 Organist paid £1.10s.0d per quarter.

1898 Organ blower at 6/3 per quarter.

CHAPTER 5

Education

69. Headteacher Mrs. J.C. Francis with pupils from Cwmfelinfach Junior School when the school received an Investor in People award from Mrs. Glenys Kinnock MEP. Pupils surrounding them include Hollie Coomer, Sophie Williams, Amanda Angove, Gareth Walker, Dane Whittaker, Matthew Prosser, Alice Collins, Aaron Watson and Kelvin Adams.

70. Hayley Thomas trimming the beard of County Councillor Byron Williams at a Charity Beard Shave held at Cwmfelinfach Junior School in the Summer Term of 1992. Hayley went on to become Headgirl at Pontllanfraith Comprehensive School.

71. A class of Cwmfelinfach Juniors with their teacher in 1968. This class includes pupils from Ynysddu. At that time Ynysddu children started school in their own village, went to the Junior School in Cwmfelinfach from the age of 8 to 11 then returned to Ynysddu for their secondary education.

72. Forty Ynysddu Infants School children with their class teacher (inset) in 1931. The Infants School was pulled down some 20 year ago, one year before it was due to celebrate its centenary.

73. The pupils in Class 4 at Bryn Primary School in 1985. Back row: Mr. Robert Bloxham, Keirion Poole, Andrew Line, Kevin Waite, David Button, Gavin Lewis, Michael Coombes, Philip Hamer, Geraint Griffiths, Mr. Douglas Munday (headteacher).Third row: Lee James, Robert Phillips, Gary Williams, Kathryn Game, Karen Moore, Eleanor Williams, Andrew Link, Ian Hayter, Andrew Rackham. Seated: Sarah Hancock, Joanne Button, Lucy Purves, Leanne Pugh, Jessica Oakley, Katy Owens, Suzanne Jones, Leanne Johnson. In front: Adam Churchward, Jeremy Jenkins, Thomas Giles, Nathan Beech.

74. The pupils in Class 7 at Bryn Primary School in 1990. Back row: Mr. Malcolm Abraham (headteacher), Andrew Fenner, Stephen Tiley, Richard Gwyn Jones, Paul Morris, Martin Ware, Rhys James, Andrew Moore, Miss Jenny Williams. Third row: Sarah Morris, Julie Kaszubowski, Chemaine Challenger, Elizabeth Millington, Claire Edwards, Lucy Martin, Caroline Walker, Sian Rackham. Seated: Joanne Hook, Carys Edwards, Sarah Jones, Elinor Bray, Sarah Cloudsdale, Claire Seabourne, Andrea Lane, Heidi Phillips, Lisa Oliver. In front Matthew Pitman, Christopher Stone, Christopher Maguire.

75. The staff at Cefn Fforest Junior School, 1989-90. Standing: Jo Kelly, Jon Murphy, Lesley Woodward, Sarah Hobbs, Paul Harrington, Trudi Partner, Val Nancollis. Seated: Robin Eyles, Moira Bancroft, Bryan Hemmings, Sheila Thayer, Christine Edwards, Sally Davies.

76. Blackwood Infants and Junior School pupils at Cefn Road School c1930.

Some entries from the Blackwood school log book of yesteryear:

7 Feb 1877 I learned that Mr T Jones, newly appointed school master was to commence on 19 Feb. Did not like the treatment. There should only be one head in one room. I did not want to submit to him nor would I expect him to submit to me.

3 May New school opened by Laybourne, president. 178 children walked from Drill Hall starting about 12 noon. They sang in new school. Key handed by architect to Chairman of the Board to Chairman of the Committee and then to me.

8 May Admitted 50 new scholars.

7 July Child had a bad fall. Much blood. Plastered and sent home.

Holidays 13 July Mid-day. To reopen 6 August.

13 Aug Several children fell in playground. Parents made complaints.

11 Sept Received teacher and monitors in own home for instruction.

26 Sept Gallery lessons given - a Tallow Candle, Sealing Wax, Loaf Sugar, Brown Sugar, Salt, A Sheep, A Cat, Wool, Feathers, Down Fur, The Printer, The Blind Woman.

24 Sept David Tillott removed from gallery for fighting. Gave him a pat on each side of the head. His mother came soon after school - shook her fist in my face, threatened, swore, and abused one in a manner not only vulgar and rude but indecent and disgusting. I wrote a note to Dr. James informing him of the circumstances and also stated that I intend to summon the woman before the magistrates.

27 Sept Obtained a summons as above.

18 Oct A holiday to enable the mistress and teachers to attend at Police Court, Mrs. Tillott having summoned mistress for assault which was dismissed at her own call. She had to pay a fine plus costs in case against herself of assault on the mistress.

3 Dec Kindergarten dispensed with as a punishment to noisy children.

7 Jan 1878 Reopened. Only 54 present. Younger children do not attend well during the winter.

Government Report - Mixed School

> Arithmetic. Good in first standard. Handwriting and spelling - only fair.
>
> Tone and discipline - good
>
> Infants. Reading good. Arithmetic fair.
>
> My lords will expect considerable improvements in the discipline of the Infants' School. Grant claimed of £91.6.11 which after deductions of £6.13.4 for staff gave balance claimed of £84.13.7

7 March Only 34 present. 26 away with measles. Several have left area to seek work.

5 June Lewis Lewis drunk, bad language again. Flourished a stick. Saw Mr. Morris that night. Police to be brought in.

26 August Mrs. Tillott abusive on road again. Her boy kept in.

6 Sept Saw Cecilia Holder about yesterday afternoon. Went to Maesycwmmer to an Eisteddfod. She went even though refused permission.

12 Sept Only two pupils turned up. Day of the Agricultural Show.

14 Oct Mistress present but not well enough to take an active part in the work of the school.

21 Nov Several children 6 years old do not know the alphabet.

26 Nov Much chicken pox.

10 Dec Whooping Cough.

11 Dec Too cold for pupils to go into playground.

8, 9, 10 Jan 1879 Deep snow.

28 Jan Best elder girls seem to stay away when there is sewing.

7 Feb Bad roads. Many prevented attending by want of shoes, their father's being out of work. Others cannot pay the school fees.

11 Feb A little boy Tommy Dodd threw a stone and broke a window in the Mixed School.

19 May Several children sent home for their fees. Some returned, their parents could not pay them. Some brought fees, others remained away.

3 June Much poverty among the children.

13 Oct Commenced duties as Mistress of Blackwood Infant School today having formerly kept Manmoel School under the same Board.

4 Nov Funeral of George E Davies employed at the school.

15 Dec Pupil teachers brought the intelligence that John George Smith was dead - one of the younger scholars.

21 Jan 1880 Caught two boys swearing. Gave class a lecture on it.

3 Aug Several new scholars from Ladies' School.

7 Sept Very hot - girl fainted.

10 Sept Several children gone to pick blackberries.

6 Dec Several families leaving the area.

Jan 1881 School closed for several days - bad snow.

23 Feb Organ opening services at church.

Easter Holiday - 1 week

24 Aug Punished Willie Price for taking money from his father's pocket. Wrote to parents.

13 Sept Two scholars went to America.

19 Oct Commenced school earlier in the morning and dismissed sooner and went to see the Royal saloon passing.

30 Nov Two men called at the school asking for charity. Several children frightened owing to their rough appearance.

17 Feb 1882 Willy Alderman fell into the fender and hurt his face but escaped from burning.

23 June Scholar died after a short illness. Parents leaving area.

23 Nov Funeral of a scholar.

12 Feb 1883 All children from Mynyddislwyn sent home it being decided that they were to attend the schools in their own parish. Some parents begged to take them back.

13 Feb Child died of measles.

20 Feb Three more died of measles.

6 March Nearly all have measles.

15 June - 16 July Summer holidays.

17 Sept Children kept at home with 'a distemper of the blood or itches'.

1 Oct John Jones died of scarlet fever.

29 Oct Miss B. Powell put in charge on 23rd. Mrs Edwards too ill.

1 Nov Mrs. Edwards died - funeral on 6th Nov. Bessie Powell 2nd Class, 3rd Division, certified teacher, has been appointed mistress of this school by the Finance Committee of the Board.

25 Jan Received 6 yds calico, $3^{1}/2$ lb knitting cotton and 4 doz. knitting pins from Mr. Morris

Lessons for 1884.

> Class I Mat weaving, Embroidery, Corkwork, Recitation, Singing and Marching.
> Class II Embroidery, Stickplaiting, Recitation, Singing, Marching.
> Class III Threading beads and Marching.

24 Feb Letter from Mr. Dauncey - Bibles and Testaments to be read each morning from 9 - 9.30. Does not apply in Infants Schools.

18 Aug Half-day. Liberal Demonstration in the Park. (This is probably Woodfield Park, the home of the Moggridge family who were Whigs, that is Liberals.)

12 Sept 101 on books. Average attendance 75.6

20 Oct Sent Isaiah Thomas (one of 1st Class boys) home as he had a ringworm in his head.

23 Oct Dr. James always gives Bessie Powell time off.

Summary of Inspector's Report for the Infants Department 1884.

This is in good order and every branch of work is receiving skillful attention. The very satisfactory exams pursued by the second class and the larger section of the first class holds out the prospect of a more decided success at an early date, unless the school suffers from the temporary loss of the classroom. If the attendance of the infants were more regular both rooms would be constantly required. The desk accommodation for writing and occupations should be increased. The Good Merit Grant and Grants for Singing by Notes and for Sewing of the Boys as well as of the girls are deserved.

Their lordships observe that the average attendance of the Infants has fallen considerably and although there are nearly 100 infants on the books My Lords would suggest the great desirability of adding another Infants classroom. Pupil Teacher C.A. Morgan has passed well. My Lords regret that the state of health of Pupil Teacher Lewis renders it necessary to remove her name from the register of Pupil Teachers serving in this school.

17 June 1885 Confirmation service in Church. Tea party at one of the chapels.

1 Sept Sent Abraham Stevens, a 1st class boy, home on account of his brother recovering from typhoid fever. He had been running the roads for the last six weeks.

7 Oct Teachers gave up sewing at 5.30 - Too dark to see any longer.

1 April 1889 School closed for a month epidemic of measles.

19 July - 12 August Summer holiday (This is the first time that the holiday has gone into August).

7 Nov 1890 Edward Alderman (in 3rd class) kicked in face by a horse, could not attend school.

7 Sept 1891 Letter from the Clerk. They have decided to make Elementary Education in their schools free.

23 Oct Several children left neighbourhood owing to stoppage in the colliery.

13 Jan 1893 Mary E. Rees to be kept on as Assistant Teacher at a salary of £40 p.a.

13 Sept 1895 Pupil broke leg, timber fell on her, dropped by the workmen who were busy altering the building.

18 Oct Martha Edwards and Albert Edwards have stayed at home because of sores breaking out all over them and even their finger nails are coming off.

2 Nov Mabon's Day. Football match in the village.

20 Jan 1897 George Henry Davies (aged 6) burnt himself to death by carrying about a candle.

8 Oct School closed for 4 weeks due to infectious diseases.

77. Pupils and Staff at Blackwood School, Pentwyn Road when it was opened in the early 1900s. The open areas beneath the classrooms, which were intended for recreational purposes during inclement weather, were subsequently sealed off and used for storage and a library. The school closed early in 2001, the town's Junior School pupils moving to new buildings at Apollo Way where they joined their younger brothers and sisters in the Infants School.

78. Miss Martin with her pupils at the wooden school in Oakdale c1931. Back row: Maldwyn Williams, Murray Williams, T. Haddock, G. Jones, J. Lane, H. Williams, B. Sims, Violet, M. Rees. Third row: H. Carter, M. Searchfield, R. Birch, M. Dutton, Adams, unknown, unknown, Dennis, D. Johnson, S. Bright, R. Williams, unknown. Second row: unknown, P. Jones, J. Payne, unknown, unknown, Robinson, Parr, D. John, J. Evans, K. Waite, I. Webb. Front row: unknown, G. Matthews, D. Hendy, S. Parfitt, H. Taylor, C. Jones, M. Hacker, unknown, T. Bradford, Morgan, A. Young.

79. Miss Olwyn Phillips (Later Mrs Hemmings) with Standard I pupils at Oakdale School c1932. Back row: D. Stephens, P. Hamer, G. Jones, B. Clancy, D. Hendy, J. Evans, I. Webb, M. Lewis, unknown, T. Brace. Third row: J. Lane, M. Hacker, P. Williams, F. Jones, C. Jones, Naomi, unknown, M. Morgan, R. Hearn, unknown. Second row: N. Taylor, G. Matthews, G. Thomas, S. Parfitt, B. Richards, M. Williams, T. Morgan, T. Haddock, D. Johnson, unknown. Front row (kneeling): unknown, T. Bradford, Morgan, Dennis, S. Bright, A. Young, R. Williams, unknown, M. Searchfield, Gravenor, H. Carter.

80. The pupils in Class 2 at Cefn Road Infants School, Blackwood, in the 1920s. The school was opened in 1877 and closed in 1980.

81. A class of 8-year-olds at Cefn Road Infants, Blackwood, c1954. With them on the left is Miss Perkins the headmistress and Miss Jenkins their teacher.

82. A class of pupils from Blackwood Junior School with their gas masks, c1940. The group includes Lal Holvey, Clifford Davies, Ronnie Williams, Jeanette Morgan, Enid Griffiths, Gordon Leach, Gordon King, Graydon Oakley and Margaret Baker.

83. Mr. Roger Price's class in Blackwood Junior School in the Summer term of 1974. Back row: Stephen Cook, Richard Jones, Adrian Lloyd, Malcolm Isles, Unknown, Christopher Corp, Carl Weaver. Middle row: Stephen Woolley, Ian, Gillian Evans, Terry-Ann Morris, Sue Evans, Paula Travers, Timothy Perry, Adrian Stone. Seated: Amanda Owen, Janet Richards, Janet Walker, Kathryn Smith, Debbie Silcocks, Tania Jewczuk, Pat Gregory. In front: Nigel, Jeffery Baker.

84. Miss Hilda Richards with her class at Cefn Fforest Infants School, in the early 1920s. School did not appear to be a very happy place in those days. Were they all forbidden to smile?

85. Prince Edward with pupils of Cwmfelinfach Junior School when he visited Ynyshywel Country Park. He is being shown the school's Queen's Jubilee Pond Project by Carly Prosser, Adrian Whatley, Hayley Thomas and Matthew Arnold assisted by several other pupils including Kate Harrhy, Emma Griffiths and John Westwood.

86. Miss Joan Abraham with her class at Cefn Fforest Junior School, 1962-63. How happy these pupils look. Compare them with those in the same school several decades earlier as shown on the facing page.

87. Six young angels! Markham Nursery School Christmas Concert 1993. Cefyn Attewell, Louise Williams, Kayleigh Jones, Yasmin Lynch, Rhian Wyatt (standing). Mark Skirpan (kneeling).

88. Markham School Reception Class, Saint David's Day 1987. Back row: Thomas Weeks, Michael Carey, Andrew Edwards, Nathan Box, Gavin Wake, Gavin Carroll, Ian Morgan. Middle row: Louise Edwards, Carla Thomas, Hayley Davies, Victoria Hughes, Kellyanne Burton, Rhiannon Withey, Vicki Edwards. Front row: Lisa Phillips, Kelly Rawle, Emma Farr, Suzanne Woszczycki, Becky Jones, Ceinwen Watkins.

89. Markham Primary School, Year 6, 1990. Back row: Mr. Holly (headmaster) Khristopher Weeks, Malcolm Perry, Mark Jones, Christopher Morgan, Leon Bryant, Kristian Lewis, Lee Griffiths, Clinton Samuels, Mr. Griffin. Middle row: Melanie Reynolds, Stacey Chamberlain, Sian Williams, Helen Payne, Donna White, Matthew Lawrence, Austen Morgan, Dale Williams, Kris Williams, Cellan Jones. Front row: Stephen Pember, Robert Jones, Danielle Lee, Rachael Edwards, Sherie Webley, Tracy Price, Michael Carey, Marcus Dix.

90. A group of girls from Oakdale with their teacher Miss Marjorie Love at a school camp in Rhoose in 1936. The back row includes Megan Rees (1), Margaret Angett (4), Lily Whiting (5), Margaret Williams (6); Third row: Gwyneth Lewis (1), Vera Jones (2), Megan Roberts (3). Second row: Peggy Williams (2), Thelma Mountney (3), Nesta Hall (4), Minnie Morris (6), Ruth Sumption (8). Front row: Linda Walker (2), Hilda Taylor (3), Joan Evans (4).

91. The girls from Class 7B at Oakdale school in 1936. Frances Edmunds, Gwyneth Matthews, Mavis Lewis, Gwyneth Biggs, Morris, Nash, Dorcas Martin, Elaine Hughes, Bronwen Morgan, Megan Roberts, Lisa Hall, Thelma M., Olive Wanklin, Olive Wilson, Violet Johnson, Betty Jeffries, Muriel Davies, Vera Farr, Hilda Clayfield, Ruth Simpkins, M.G. Lewis, Grace Jones, Doreen Williams, Vera Jones.

92.

93.

94.
92.-94. Staff and pupils at Pontllanfraith Grammar School c1953.

The topography and industry of the valleys of Western Monmouthshire was such that in the 1880s there were four north/south railway lines joined by an east/west line across the top of these valleys and another across the bottom. In the north there were stations at Rhymney, Tredegar, Ebbw Vale and Nantyglo, while in the south the stations were at Maesycwmmer, Pontllanfraith, Newbridge and Pontypool. By 1890 it was obvious that there was a great need for grammar schools to assist in the education of the rapidly growing population and so in 1891 a county scheme proposed that a grammar school should be built near each of the eight places where the six railway lines crossed. In the first phase Grammar schools were built at Abertillery 1896, Tredegar 1896, Pontypool (girls) 1897, Ebbw Vale 1897, Abergavenny (girls) 1898 and Pontywaun 1898.

Students from Blackwood who did not attend Lewis' School, Pengam or Lewis' School, Hengoed travelled to Tredegar but the population of Tredegar was expanding so rapidly that the accommodation in Tredegar was needed solely for local pupils. As it stood, places were needed at Tredegar for 450+ pupils but only 240 places were available. A new school was proposed at Pontllanfraith. This was a convenient spot about half way between the existing schools used by Sirhowy Valley pupils, one at Tredegar and another at Pontywaun and would be near a main railway junction.

The site for the school had been bought for £3113 in 1911 but there was a protracted wrangle between the County Council and the Tredegar Iron Company over a pit railway or aerial tipping line which the company wanted to pass over a corner of the proposed site. By 1922 - 11 years later! - the company finally got the message that the council would not give way. In June 1923 plans were drawn up for a Central School for 252 pupils. Central schools reflected experiments with different types of schools which had been sought for some time. The objective of these schools was 'to prepare children for a life of active labour and social cooperation'. The school leaving age, which had been 13 since 1870, was raised to 14 in 1921 and this was going to present additional accommodation problems. The plans were submitted to the Board of Education and approved in the September. However, a letter from the Tredegar Group Manager to the Education Committee stressed the lack of secondary education in the Sirhowy Valley and urged for a secondary school instead of the proposed central school. The Board of Education rejected this suggestion. In December 1924 a construction tender for £21,000 was accepted and in January 1925 the Board sanctioned costs of £22,500 for accommodation for 188 pupils. It was arranged to admit 88 pupils in September - 49 to be transferred from the secondary schools at Tredegar and Newbridge and a further 39 to be admitted by an entrance examination. The County Council went ahead with the Central School at Pontllanfraith convinced that it would become the Grammar School that the area needed and in the hope that when the school was ready it would be recognised as a Grammar School. By the time the school opened, attitudes at central government had changed and the school opened its doors as Pontllanfraith Grammar School. By 1939 the number of pupils on role had increased to 244. In due course the local Junior Technical School, which had started in 1926, merged with the grammar school to give Pontllanfraith Grammar Technical School which subsequently became the Pontllanfraith Comprehensive School we know today.

Those seated in photographs 92 to 94 are, from the left

92. Melville Edwards, Lewis Gravenor, Warren Phillips, Caryl Eustace, Karl Esau (head boy), Mr. Baker (caretaker), Mr. Edgar Phillips (RI and Welsh), Mr. Walter Sweet (Mathematics), Mr. Walters (French), Mr. Edgar Bond (Art), Mr. Barton (Music).

93. Mr. Ron Glencross (French), Mr. Haydn Howells (Art), Mr. Dan Williams (Chemistry), Mr. Tom Garrett (Physics), Mr. John Capwell (deputy headmaster, Latin), Mr. Cliff Rowlands (headmaster). Miss M.G. Phillips (Senior Mistress, History), Miss J.M. England (Biology), Miss Linda Bowditch (Geography), Miss M. Phillips (English), Mrs. J.C. Hibbins (Mathematics).

94. Miss Sheila Fenessy (French), Mrs. Salmon (PE), Mrs. Baker (school cook), Mrs. Marjorie Edwards (secretary), Beryl Rose (head girl), Joyce Thomas, Jean Powell, Jean Barnett, Margaret Houghton, Joan Morgan, Shirley Evans.

CHAPTER 6

Industry, Trade and Transport

95. Wyllie colliery was the last deep mine to be sunk in the lower Sirhowy Valley, following Oakdale in 1908 and Markham in 1912. Trial sinkings were made at Gelligroes in 1900 but had to be abandoned because of excessive water. Preparatory work was eventually started in December 1923 and by the end of the following year work had begun on the engine houses and other buildings in accordance with the layout planned by A.S. Tallis and implemented by Messrs. William Angus Scott the consulting engineers. Two shafts were sunk 50 yards apart, each 20 feet in diameter. Boring continued at just over 8 yards a day until they got to the steam coals. The sinkers, Piggott and Sons, bored the North shaft to a depth of 598 yards and the South shaft 31 yards deeper. The whole operation at Wyllie was made easier by the lessons that had been learned at Markham a decade earlier, but an unexpected fact was that the borings went through just two seams of coal instead of the expected five. What is more, it was not clear how these seams were related to those already previously worked at adjacent collieries. Due to the limitations of the site and the lack of an adequate water supply the colliery was wholly electric. Underground cables were laid from the power house at Oakdale, which also supplied the power for its own needs and that of nearby Markham.

In 1929, by which time the colliery had been operational for three years, it took 3.1 tons of coal to produce enough power to raise 100 tons of coal to the surface. This was considered to be most efficient. The size of the workforce increased rapidly reaching its maximum of 900 in 1935. A small village of 200-250 mainly semi-detached houses was planned to the north of the colliery but whatever the reason only about 110 were ever built. Although Wyllie was hailed as a modern colliery it was not modern enough to have a pithead baths. Miners had to wait until 1947 before they could avail themselves of this luxury.

96. Nine Mile Point Colliery, Cwmfelinfach. Coronation Colliery, known later as Nine Mile Point, was sunk in 1902 and operated initially as Burnyeat and Brown. It was subsequently owned by the Ocean Coal Company prior to nationalisation in 1947. During sinking operations in 1904 seven sinkers were killed by a landslide. The colliery had three shafts; the Rock Vein pit went down six hundred feet into the Upper Coal Measures while the east and west shafts went down twice that distance into the Middle and Lower Coal Measures. In 1913 2,105 men were employed at the colliery. A strike began on Saturday 12 October 1935 when 78 men remained underground as a result of 'scab' labour in the form of members of the South Wales Miners Industrial Union being brought in from outside the area. At the end of the following week 30,000 miners in the coal field were on strike. The problem was settled after many of the men had been underground for 177 hours. Nine Mile Point Colliery was nationalised and in the early 1960s the National Coal Board spent £2.5 million to modernise the pit only to close it suddenly in 1964 when resistance appeared weakest.

97. Abernant Colliery, Markham. This colliery, which was situated to the east of the main Blackwood/Tredegar road below the village of Markham, was sunk in the 1880s by the Bargoed Coal Company. There were two shafts as far as the Brithdir seam. The colliery employed 483 men in 1913, ceased mining in 1932, but two years later still employed ten men, four of whom were underground, on maintenance and pumping operations. The colliery was linked underground with the nearby Llanover Colliery, which was a little further down the valley.

98. Markham Colliery as it looked in 1919. Sinking began in 1911 and the pit became operational in 1912. When the pit first opened the average weekly miner's wage was 5/- (25p) but an all-out strike in that year resulted in a minimum wage being introduced from 1914.

99. Markham Colliery in the early 1980s. This was taken a few years before it closed in 1986. All that remains on the site today are the capped shafts.

100. A pre-1920 photograph of Oakdale Colliery from the main Blackwood - Tredegar road.

101. This photograph shows a clean and relatively newly painted colliery at Oakdale in April 1990, just months before the whole enterprise closed down. The site was then cleared fairly quickly. Today part of the ground has been used for housing and the remainder is being laid out for business and industrial purposes.

102. A view of the coal cleaning plants at Oakdale colliery looking towards the North-west. This photograph was taken from the top of Number 2 chimney in 1939 while the plants were in the process of construction. The centre of the photograph shows the building of Number 2 washery; just above which is the 'rubbish' bridge over the River Sirhowy. This bridge was made in the colliery tram shop.

103. A photograph which shows demolition in progress at Oakdale Colliery in June 1990. The north shaft headgear lies in a tangled heap on the ground while the south shaft headgear still stands.

104. Tom Morgan with Simon Life, the Shift Charge Engineer (Mechanical) in front of the north shaft of Oakdale Colliery in August 1989, the year before demolition.

105. The back of the baths at Oakdale colliery as the building appeared from the north west in June 1989. The ground floor was the lamp room. These baths had been built c1950 and were in continuous use until the colliery closed in 1990. Today there are houses on the site.

106. Members of Oakdale No 2 Rescue Team on a training course at Crumlin Rescue Station in 1977. Back row: D. Hawkins, M. Phillips, B. Lloyd, Nick, the full-time training instructor. Front row: T. Morgan, L. Coyle, C. Bram. Because there were over a thousand men at the colliery two rescue teams were required. No 1 team also had six members.

107. The Powell Duffryn tip in Aberbargoed pre-1939. This was one of the largest coal tips in Europe and completely obstructed a view of Bargoed from properties along the main road. Note the height of the tip compared with the horse in the foreground. In recent years this tip has been almost wholly removed. What remains has been carefully landscaped so that there is a pleasing aspect of Bargoed across the valley.

108. Mynyddislwyn Number One Oakdale Rescue Party. (Date unknown)

109. The 1926 strike brought the country to a very low ebb but nowhere more so than in the mining valleys of South Wales. Soup kitchens and Distress Funds were set up almost everywhere. This Statement of Accounts shows the receipts and payments for the Markham Distress Fund until it was wound up in February 1927. There was cash in hand at the beginning of the strike from a previous occasion but the fund was completely exhausted by the time of this statement.

RECEIPTS

	£. s. d	£. s. d
CASH IN HAND FROM PREVIOUS DISTRESS FUND (Per Markham Institute and Library)		12. 5. 8
SUBSCRIPTIONS:-		
Markham Colliery Officials etc	318.10. 6	
Bedwellty U.D.Council Employees	41. 5. 8	359.16. 2
DONATIONS:-		
Whist Drive Committee	30.16.11	
Sports Committee	14.10. 0	
Markham Glee Party	14. 0. 0	
Concert(Party)Committee	7. 4. 0	
Markham Labour Party	5. 0. 0	
Boxing Committee	4.11. 0	
Markham Colliery Examiners	3. 3. 0	
Markham School Staff	2.17. 0	
Blackwood Relief Committee	2.16. 0	
S. Challenger Esq., Bedwellty	2. 2. 0	
Jack Lewis Esq., Bedwellty	1.10. 0	
V. A. Tallis Esq., Tredegar	1. 5. 0	
Dance Committee	1. 4. 8	
Markham Conservative Association	1. 4. 0	
Hollybush Male Voice Party	1. 1. 0	
Dr. J. Griffiths, Argoed	1. 1. 0	
W. D. Woolley Esq., Tredegar	1. 0. 0	
"Anonymous"	1. 0. 0	
E. Williams Esq., Aberdare	1. 0. 0	
Revd. Davies, Bedwellty	10. 0	
W. Adams Esq., New Tredegar	10. 6	
Mrs. Evan Lewis, Blackwood	10. 0	
Markham Girl Guides	10. 0	
T. Pritchard Esq., Oakdale	5. 0	
Bedwellty R.A.O.B., Victory Lodge	5. 0	
Cohen Esq., Tredegar	5. 0	
Cavanagh Esq., Tredegar	5. 0	
P.C. Grande, Markham	2. 6	100. 5. 7
COLLECTIONS:-		
Carnivals,Cricket & Football Matches	6.11. 3	
Made at Manmoel	2. 6. 0	
" " Markham Buildings	1. 2. 5	
" " Markham Village	13. 0	10.12. 8
		£ 483. 0. 1

PAYMENT

	£. s. d	£. s. d
PROVISIONS ETC.		
Mrs R. Powell, Markham	126.10. 6	
T.Foulkes & Co	45. 2. 4	
Tredegar Industrial & Provident Society, Tredegar..............	43. 3. 7	
Hill Stores, Tredegar	28.16. 7	
C. Bartlett	2. 0.10	245.13.10
MEATS		
John Morgan & Sons, Markham		126. 2. 2
GREEN GROCERY ETC.:-		
D.C. Phillips, Hollybush	18.16.11	
Wyndham-Pugh, Blackwood	9. 2. 3	
Wright & Lodge, Tredegar	7. 7. 6	
Oakey Bros	6. 7. 0	
L. E. Thomas, Markham	1. 9. 6	
Sundries (Potatoes)	11. 0	43.14. 2
MILK		
Woolworths	6. 0	
D. Lewis, Hollybush	51.11. 4	51.17. 4
DONATION TO HOLLYBUSH DISTRESS FUND		3. 0. 0
BANK CHARGES	1. 8. 0	
Less Refund for unused cheques	1. 1. 4	1. 6. 8
SUNDRIES		
Fuel, Oil etc	1. 1. 3	
Cleaning hut		
Mrs Hanley	2. 6	
P.Callaghan & W.Burke	5. 0	
Mrs R. Thomas	5. 0	
Mrs T. Watkins	3.11	
Travelling Expenses (bus fares)	16. 5	
Whist Drive Prizes	15. 0	
Repairs to Chairs	13. 0	
Donation to Church for use of hut	10. 0	
Cooking utensils, Glass etc	8. 9	
Stationery	7. 6	5. 1.11
GRATUITIES TO MESSRS. S. KNOCK, P. CALLAGHAN etc		6. 4. 0
		£ 483. 0. 1

110. The entrance to Woodfield Colliery, near the Rock and Fountain public house, Blackwood, showing several miners standing behind full trams. A truck stands in the adjacent sidings waiting to be loaded with the coal from these trams. No trace of this enterprise remains today.

111. Tuckers was the principal butchery business on Blackwood High Street pre-1920. This photograph shows their shop around 1920. It was situated on the corner opposite Poundstretcher. The side window of the shop on the other side of the alley (Jones and Porter's the grocers in the 1950s) has long since been blocked up. Note the distinctive stonework at the boundaries of the frontage, and the number of people employed. The hygiene regulations of the day were obviously rather different from those of today! This is where A.J. Brown (see photograph 113) was employed until he set up his own business in a shed below Albion Terrace, moving to the shop adjacent to the Gulf Garage (later Ellaways the hairdresser) c1925.

112. Meat on the hoof arriving at Woodwards the butchers in the 1930s. The animal would be killed in the slaughterhouse behind the High Street. There were no long journeys to abattoirs in those days when most of the meat sold was bred and reared locally.

113. Brown's the butchers as it first looked. Note the telephone number. Two digits were enough in those days.

114. The same premises in the 1980s. The business now belongs to Ossie Brown, one of the sons, and his son Stewart who has carried on the business up to the present day. It was commonplace in bygone decades to find customers queuing on to the pavement on a Friday and on a Saturday morning.

115. The railway station at Ynysddu. This was part of the London and North West Railway Company's system.

116. Pontllanfraith station c1958 showing the bridge over the line, the two signal boxes and the level crossing with the gates closed to traffic. Standing on the down line is an auto-train. The engine was always on the top side (Tredegar side) of the coach. When the train was going down the valley (as here), the driver was in a cab at the far end of the coach while the fireman was on the engine. When the train came up the valley both driver and fireman travelled on the engine.

117. A train at Pontllanfraith Top Station c1955 waiting to travel north to Blackwood on its journey to Tredegar. This station was known as Tredegar Junction until its name was changed to Pontllanfraith in July 1911. Apart from a double decker bus there is no traffic on the Pontllanfraith/Blackwood road behind. The timber building between the bus and the train is a new booking office. This was needed in place of the original office whose roof was blown off by a gas explosion when a gas lamp was lit in October 1952. In the shop with the sun blind you could buy almost anything at any time, even fish and chips! It was affectionately known as Fanny Grabits and served the local community well before the days of the supermarket.

118. Blackwood station from the north c1958. Note the wooden platform which was an extension to the original platform.

119. A view of the main signal box and railway station at Blackwood from the town side c1958. The station was always considered to be a long way from the town centre and so not used for passenger traffic as much as it might have been, particularly with the advent of a public bus service.

120. A view, looking towards Blackwood, of a train standing on the down line in Pontllanfraith Top Station c1958.

121. A picture of Fleur-de-lys station, on the Brecon and Merthyr line, taken from a train on a pleasant summer's afternoon c1958.

122. Pontllanfraith Bottom Station from the west platform looking towards Crumlin c1955.

123. Sleepy Blackwood High Street one afternoon in the late 1960s. The businesses nearest the camera are D.J. Evans (grocer), Jordans (boots and shoes), Restighini's café, Browns (butchers) and Briggs (boots and shoes).

124. The Crown Public House, The Bryn, Pontllanfraith is more than one hundred and fifty years old. A coroner's inquest on the death of Edward Barnes a 15-year old boy was held there as long ago as 14 February 1857. He had been killed by a brick that had been thrown at another man who was accused of stealing coal. The post mortem was carried out by Mr. Leigh, Llanvabon.

125. A West Mon double decker bus (Number 14, Reg. 203 CWO) passing through The Square, Blackwood, in the late 1960s. The bus was a Leyland/Massey 55-seater bought in 1962 and withdrawn in 1979. It was renumbered 33, became the driver training vehicle, and was the last double-decker to be sold, being towed from the depot on 22 January 1982. Glyn Lewis's radio and television business is adjacent to the Gas showroom. Behind the bus the Crown public house and Ceph Stewart's newspaper business have recently given way to Tesco. Tesco remained open until May 2001.

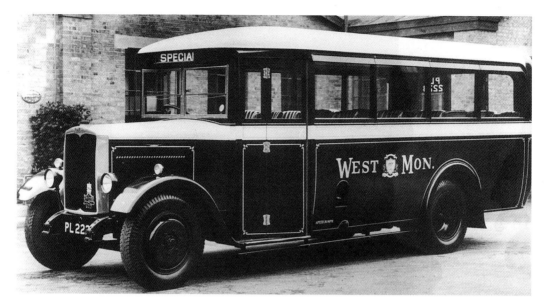

126. A twenty-seater Leyland Cub bus, Registration Number PL 2223, with Leyland bodywork. This vehicle was built in 1930 by Leyland Motors and used as their demonstrator until it was bought by the West Monmouthshire Omnibus Board in February 1931. The 'Cub' was a new model at the time and PL 2223 was one of the first 'Cubs' to be built. In 1937 this bus was specially decorated to celebrate the Coronation of King George VI.

127. The last regular board meeting of the West Monmouthshire Omnibus Board was held on 4th March 1974. From its birth in 1926 the company had been operated jointly by the councils of Bedwellty and Mynyddislwyn. Standing: B. Mantle (Bedwellty), G.C. Garrett (Bedwellty), E.J. Butler (Bedwellty), T.J. Duckham (Mynyddislwyn). Seated G.H. Coleman FCIT (General Manager and Chief Financial Officer), J.D. Turner (Bedwellty) Vice Chairman, A.G. Mayo (Mynyddislwyn) Chairman, Mrs M.R. Powell (Bedwellty), D. Leslie Davies Solicitor (Clerk to the board). Absent: H. Lewis (Bedwellty), C.C. Thomas (Mynyddislwyn).

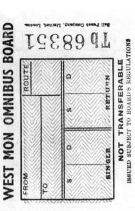

Fh 5702   9284   D 7763   5237

128. These five bus tickets, the first four of which belonged to the Willebrew system, were originally used on local buses in the 1920s. The first is a Lewis & James ticket, the largest company operating in the district at that time and formed in 1920. The second ticket was issued by the Blackwood Motor Company and is probably the oldest ticket. This company was taken over by the Griffin Motor Co. of Brynmawr, who issued the third ticket. The fourth was issued by The Western Services Ltd. They operated buses from Tredegar to Newport and Blackwood to Pontypool. The James and Lewis ticket has an advertisement for Jones & Porter's Groceries and Provisions on the back while Blackwood Motor Services ticket advertises A.P. Hughes the Blackwood Draper. Lewis and James's ticket shows that for the route to which it applied there were nineteen stops. The conductor punched the number corresponding to the bus stop where the passenger got on; the left hand numbers referred to the outward journey and the right hand numbers to the inward journey. Of the other tickets one has numbers from 0 to 35 and another from 1 to 40. All four tickets had been printed by Williamson of Ashton-under-lyne. The fifth ticket is an example of a Bell Punch ticket which was used from the 1940s until 1971.

West Monmouthshire Omnibus
STOPPAGE !

In view of the stoppage which is greatly inconveniencing the General Public, the West M.O.B., Employees announce the fact that **they are prepared to discuss the causes of the dispute at any meeting** which may be called for by **any member of the Public.**

We have at all times held ourselves ready to negotiate with the Board, and have on several occasions made definite approaches with the purpose of bringing about an immediate resumption of work. On Sunday, December 23rd, 1945 Mr. D. T. Jones, M.P. for West Hartepool together with Mr. A. V. Nichols, Secretary of the Pontypridd Branch attempted to act as intermediaries in the dispute.

The suggestions made by Mr. Jones, as a fair basis for negotiation were accepted by the men but were **rejected by the Board.** Despite the Board's rejection of Mr. Jones' offer, the men have since made repeated attempts to open negotiations.

In a dastardly attempt to intimidate their employees, **The Board issued notices on Christmas Eve to terminate the employment of every man,** which reads as follows :—

" **WEST MONMOUTHSHIRE OMNIBUS BOARD**

Notice is hereby given to each employee of the Board who is now wrongfully withholding his services to the Board that unless he returns to work on or before Wednesday next the 26th instant his employment under the Board will be terminated at the expiration of one week from that date.

Dated this 24th day of December, 1945.

TREVOR C. GRIFFITHS,
Clerk to the Board."

PLEASE MAKE THIS KNOWN

Branch Secretary—**CLIFF THOMAS, 26, Commin Road, Aberbargoed**

Peter Williams, Printers, Bargoed.

129. The West Monmouthshire Omnibus Board existed from 1926 to 1974. During that period there was only one strike. This was caused because the Board wanted to appoint as inspector, a former member of the office staff who had been away serving in the armed forces. Since promotion to inspector was the only way up for a driver, most employees thought that the post should go to an existing driver. The strike lasted just over a week but the Board had their way. This stoppage notice was issued by the Transport & General Workers' Union and includes a copy of the notice sent to each employee.

130. An aerial view of the Stone House and the surrounding area c1950. At that time the building which is now the Stone House was Lane's grocery and provisions store. The Remploy factory is seen to the right but Blackwood Secondary Modern School, later to become the Comprehensive School, is yet to be built. In the foreground, covering several acres, are the business premises of Charles Morgan with its large assortment of ex-government and other vehicles. To the left of the Scrap Yard stands Ellis Morgan's lorry yard.

131. Members of the Morgan family whose ancestors had come to the area from the other side of the River Severn in the 1840s.

132. Members of the Morgan family with their principal means of transporting goods in 1932. Charles Morgan is in the centre.

133. Carpanini's shop and café in Maindee Road, Cwmfelinfach, c1920. Like most other Italian café owners in the valleys, the Carpaninis had come from Bardi. After they moved to Cwmcarn this property was taken over by Silverthorns. The adjacent shop was a cobblers.

134. Thomas the Chemists on the main street in Aberbargoed in the 1930s.

135. A selection of billheads from businesses that traded on Blackwood High Street more than fifty years ago, not one of which has survived.

136. The proprietors of Tidals Stores furnishing business with an exhibition stand c1955. Mr. Len Brown, Mr. Tidal Parsons, Mrs. Parsons, Mr. Homer, Mr. C.A.M. Bennett. This business, though now owned by Mr. Ian Edwards, still trades on Blackwood High Street.

137. Members of the staff of Islwyn Borough Council Transport Department who attended a function at at the Penllwyn Hotel, Pontllanfraith on 27th March 1977 to mark the retirement of Inspector Ron Relleen, Mrs. Dianne Jenkins and Mrs. Alison James. Standing: Elvet Williams, Terry Agland, Ron Relleen, Des Ferrier, Sandra Davenport, Terry John, Joyce Lawson, Don Jones, Lynne Davies, Gillian Evans, Gordon Redmore, Hilary Aubrey Seated: Joan Onions, Dianne Jenkins, Glyn H. Coleman (Transport Manager), Alison James.

CHAPTER 7

Sport and Entertainment

138. Blackwood Rugby Football Club, Monmouthshire 1st Division Winners 1981-82. Standing: D. Williams, J. Jenkins, G. Jones, M. Radford, T. Shaw, A. Tomsa, S. Lloyd, H. Thomas, W. Norwood, N. Turley, P. Fletcher. In front: I. Maybrey, G. Gwilt, S. Chidgey, G. Williams (Captain), G. Lewis, W. Powles, C. Davies.

139. Oakdale Rugby Football Club 1921-22.

140. Pontllanfraith Secondary School soccer team - winners of the A.P. Hughes cup in 1933. This was some years before rugby became the most important team game played in the secondary schools of South Wales. A.P. Hughes was for many years the principal draper in the town. Back row: P. Hopkins, R. Piper, R. Holmes, L. Griffiths, T. Jones. Middle row: C. James, A. Parry, E. Lewis (Captain), B. Williams, R. Hughes. Front row: R. Thomas, K. Richards. At this time the headmaster was Mr. D. Bowen, the deputy headmaster Mr. Cliff Rowlands and the sportsmaster Mr. T Rees.

141. Pontllanfraith Grammar School First Rugby XV 1949-50. Back row: Courtney Treasure, Spencer Waters, Ellis Williams, John Powell, Vernon Morgan, David Davies, Warren Phillips. Seated: Derrick Morgan, Alan Wilkins, Mr. Cliff Rowlands (Headmaster), Brian Thomas (Captain), Mr. Walter Sweet (Sportsmaster), Idris Samuels, Alan Rogers. Front row: Wilf Harries, C. Griffin, Clive Robinson, Bernard Maydwell.

142. The 1979-80 Netball Team at Blackwood Comprehensive School. Standing: Mrs. Gaynor Deeks, Paula Saralis, Linda Lee, Deborah Adams, Louise Thomas, Andrea King. Seated: Jacqueline Jones, Natasha Grey, Julie Wilson, Martina Lewis, Paula Davies.

143. Pontllanfraith Grammar School Netball team 1951-52. Standing: Unknown, Dorothy Prout, Pam Saunders, Tracey Winterson, Molly Maguire. Seated: Mr. C. Rowlands (Headmaster), Avril Hughes (Captain), Hazel Cummings, Mrs Salmon (PE teacher).

144. Pontllanfraith A.F.C. who won the Second Division of the Welsh League in 1950. Standing: Alwyn Waite, Danny Williams, Billy Reeves, Richards, Tom Purnell. Seated: Ron Thomas, Cliff Pritchard, Mervyn Gilchrist, Malcolm Watkins (mascot). In front: Reg Thomas and Ken Worman.

145. Players and officials of Pontllanfraith A.F.C. in 1949. Standing: Owen Smith, Bill Walters (trainer), Emlyn Mantle (President), Ken Jones, John Butterworth, Cecil Bodman, Frank Shore, Rev. Pickering (St. Augustine's), Billy Phipps (committee), Fred Davies. Seated: Cliff Pritchard, Mervyn Gilchrist, Ken Llewellyn, Danny Williams, Ken Elston, Reg Thomas. In front: 'Dixie' Jones and Derek Jones.

146. A party of bowlers selected from the various bowling clubs in the Sirhowy Valley who went on a tour to Weymouth in 1980. Standing: Gerald Maine, Sandy Wyatt, David Williams, Harry Clarke, David Davies, Trevor Tovey, Jim Francis, Terry Davies, Joe Gibbon, Stephen Bridge, Doug Davies, Granville Williams, Paddy Buckley, Doug Gilchrist. Seated: Ken Fletcher, Ray Webster, Dai Watkins, Gwyn Evans, Mike Way. In front: Keiron Davies, Malcolm Bidgway, John Maine, Ian Clarke, Ryan Buckley, David Jones and Terry Howells.

147. Pontllanfraith Grammar School Netball Team 1953-54. Standing: Mr. C. Rowlands (Headmaster), Dorothea Lewis, Maralyn Lambkin, Wendy Morris, Mrs. Salmon (PE teacher). Seated: Jackie Barnett, Jeanne Barnett, Dorothy Prout, Mary Davies.

148. The organisers of the Intercentre Sidecar Team Trial outside the Masonic Hall, Blackwood, on 29th March 1981. Forty-eight teams competed, each team being composed of a driver and sidecar passenger. The event was organised by members of Pontllanfraith Auto Club. From the left: John Roberts with his 146cc Jawa (Clerk of the course), Mrs. Ada Roberts (Secretary), Michael Rees, 310cc Montesa (Press Officer) and Harold Lewis, 175cc Yamaha (Assistant Clerk of the Course).

149. Members of Pontllanfraith Auto Club assembled at Ebbw Vale to compete in a Time and Observation Trial during the 1957-58 season. From the left: Charlie Skinner (350cc AJS), John Morgan (197cc James), John Roberts (197cc HJH which was manufactured in Swansea), Gomer Davies (197cc Francis Barnett), Derek Byfel (500cc Triumph).

150. Blackwood Cricket Team c1925. The team includes J.M. Lane, G. Lane and of course a Parfitt. It would be impossible to have a local cricket team of yesteryear without a Parfitt!

151. The members of the West Mon Omnibus soccer team playing at Porth on 7th September 1950. Standing: unknown, J. Pritchard, D. Prosser, W. O'Neill, H. Jenkins, W. Bram. In front: unknown, M. Watkins, T. Williams, T. Jenkins, G. Adams.

152. Members of Cefn Fforest Institute Bowling Club assembled around a corner of the green in 1935.

153. An early photograph from the archives of Cefn Fforest Cricket Club. Back row: G. Davies, C. Miller, A. Cookshaw, Herbie Marsh, J. Salaway, Danny Davies, Joey Jones. Middle row: Wyn Powell, Arthur Marsh, Bill Smith, Jack Marsh, Albert Davies. In front: Rev Seaton, Loll Smith, A. Marsh.

154. Dave Howells (left), Graham Morgan and Andrew Bullen (right) with the Talbot Sunbeam that Andrew drove in the Harry Flatters Rally on the Mynydd Epynt Military Ranges on 26th August 1985. This rally was held on roads closed to the public on rally day. The Stonehouse Garage team of McDonald/Howells and Bullen/Morgan won the team award as illustrated by the row of cups on the car roof. Stonehouse garage has been involved in preparing rally cars for more than twenty years.

155. Alan McDonald's Mark II Escort 2000 rally car being serviced on the top of Mynydd Epynt during the Harry Flatters Rally in August 1985. From the left Adrian Gibbons (bending), Chris Bowen, Dave Howells, Gordon, Dai, Alan McDonald, Adrian Bullen, Mike Bullen, Malcolm Rogers.

156. Local builder Bob Gibbons, a member of Blackwood Motor Club, pictured with his co-driver Stuart Cordell, competing in the Classic Rally of Wales organised by Swansea Motor Club in January 1999. Driving a Mark II Ford Cortina GT they won the Welsh Association of Motor Clubs Historic Rally Championship in 1999 and went on to compete in the National Historic Championship the following year where they won their class but more significantly were third overall. The car was prepared and maintained by Toby Adam (T2 Motorsport) another member of Blackwood MC. Blackwood Motor Club was established in 1994 and has a strong membership which is active in Road and Stage competitions. The club were Welsh Club Champions in 1999 and club members won the Welsh Road Rallying Championship (Gary Jones) and Welsh Tarmac Championship (Damian Cole) in 2000.

157. Allison Coleman shows off the Moulton cycle she won as first prize in the fifth annual competition held in 1966 to find Monmouthshire's Senior Safe Cycling Champion. From the left: Elizabeth White, Allison Coleman, Corinne Evans and Clive Jones. Allison had a unique record in that two years previously she had already won her first Moulton cycle when she became Junior Champion in the same competition. Other competitors from the Bedwellty and Mynyddislwyn Councils' areas in 1964 were: Robert Hardwick, Clive Pritchard, Sian Hodges, Howard Corke, Quentin Jones, Michael Yandle and Michael Jenkins.

CHAPTER 8

People and Events

Population movement into Blackwood in the mid 19th Century

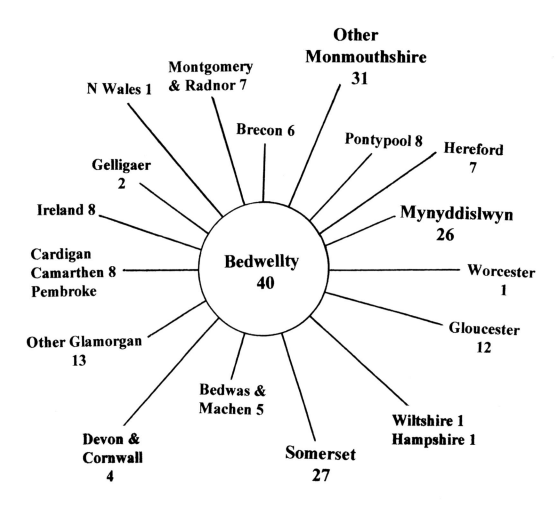

Where did our forebears come from? This diagram shows the place of birth, by parish or county, of 208 heads of household in the Blackwood area of the Parish of Bedwellty as recorded in the British census of 1881. It shows that 73 (35%) were born in or near Bedwellty parish (Mynyddislwyn, Gelligaer or Bedwas and Machen), 74 (36%) came from other parts of Wales, 53 (25%) came from England (mainly Somerset and Gloucester) and 8 (4%) from Ireland. It is significant that almost all the 'leadinglights' in the town came from some distance. The vicar was from Glamorgan, the curate Carmarthen, the headteacher North Wales, the governess Bristol, the police sergeant Gloucester, the drapers and grocers from West Wales and Gloucester, the Station master from Pembroke, the farm baillifs from Mid Wales and Somerset, a colliery manager, watchmaker, newsagent, blacksmith and rail inspector from Somerset, the boot and shoe makers from Gloucester and Somerset. Do these facts and figures support the fact that this new town was very English from an early date? Is this why the name of our town is Blackwood and not Coed Duon?

Age distribution of all persons recorded in 1881 as living in Blackwood on the day of the census.

	Under 5	5-9	10-19	20-29	30-39	40-49	50-59	60-69	70-79	80-89	Total
Males	67	61	86	57	48	41	36	24	14	3	437
Females	74	62	100	64	56	55	26	27	15	3	482
Both sexes	141	123	186	121	104	96	62	51	29	6	919

For every 1000 males the corresponding number of females is 1103.

This table shows how the population of the town (919) was distributed among the 208 inhabited properties in the town.

Number of people	0	1	2	3	4	5	6	7	8	9	10	11	12	13
Number of properties	49	18	35	34	28	31	23	15	13	5	-	3	2	1

The average number of people in each property is 4.42. The six properties with more than ten inhabitants were the large drapers and grocers shops. At that time it was the custom for many staff to 'live in'. Apart from 39 uninhabited houses the following properties are listed as unoccupied: Drill Hall, Wesley Chapel, Primitive Methodist Chapel, Welsh Baptist Chapel, Coach and Horses Inn, Royal Oak Inn, Crown Inn, Plas Farm (at the top of Gordon Road) and Cwm Gelly colliery.

Our community has always had a poor record when it comes to health. Life expectancy was never as high in this valley as in the country as a whole. As late as 1944 the number of infant deaths per thousand live births was 60.6 in the Parish of Bedwellty whereas it was 48.6 for Wales and 46 for England. By 1949 the figure had dropped to 39.5 for Wales and 32 for England but, at 59, had hardly changed for our parish. During the period 1800 to 1929 the average age at death, as indicated by the gravestones at Bedwellty church, increased from 15.2 to 68.5 years. This is not the whole story, for it omits those whose details are not given on a gravestone - often the poor and unhealthy. For all that, the following table makes interesting reading.

Age at death as recorded on gravestones at Bedwellty Church for burials between 1800-1929.

	Under 1	1-4	5-9	10-19	20-29	30-39	40-49	50-59	60-69	70-79	80-89	90+	Total	Average age at death
1800-09	3	2	1	1		1				1			9	15.2
1810-19	3		1	2	5			1	1				13	21.5
1820-29	7	2	1	2	8	2	3	4	4	2	1		36	32.1
1830-39	14	14	3	2	8	14	3	7	7	6	2	1	81	30.2
1840-49	26	37	6	10	13	8	12	8	11	10	5		146	25.6
1850-59	32	30	9	12	18	20	26	16	21	20	4	1	209	32.4
1860-69	27	37	9	17	31	12	26	24	20	16	15	4	238	35.1
1870-79	34	27	9	15	18	24	25	35	27	18	12		244	35.9
1880-89	24	39	14	21	27	20	29	28	30	40	14	3	289	38.3
1890-99	35	33	11	10	24	32	13	40	44	36	14	1	293	39.5
1900-09	2	6	2	5	13	18	13	20	35	28	26		168	55.1
1910-19	1	2		1	4	5	5	9	25	20	11	3	86	61.8
1920-29			1		2		5	5	6	17	13	2	51	68.5
Total	208	229	67	98	171	156	160	197	231	214	117	15	1863	

Rainfall (inches) in Blackwood for the period January 1968 to December 2000

Year	Jan	Feb	Mar	Apr	May	Jun	July	Aug	Sep	Oct	Nov	Dec	Total
1968	5.96	2.50	5.37	3.54	4.36	5.89	7.11	2.27	9.21	8.08	4.32	5.89	64.50
1969	**8.36**	**3.02**	**2.82**	**2.96**	**6.24**	**3.15**	**0.13**	**2.83**	**2.93**	**1.11**	**5.91**	**5.27**	**46.95**
1970	11.83	5.39	2.55	3.73	1.65	3.39	3.44	4.73	5.72	4.73	11.09	2.65	61.90
1971	10.95	2.59	3.69	2.44	4.44	4.74	0.76	8.25	1.20	4.93	3.78	3.02	50.80
1972	7.62	7.15	5.69	4.64	7.55	4.60	1.16	2.40	2.62	3.65	6.40	11.64	65.12
1973	**2.18**	**2.70**	**1.25**	**3.98**	**5.10**	**1.99**	**2.78**	**4.17**	**5.15**	**1.48**	**2.02**	**3.40**	**36.20**
1974	10.8	8.35	1.83	0.53	3.71	2.57	4.88	3.95	11.32	2.20	6.11	6.02	62.27
1975	**9.52**	**2.58**	**3.03**	**2.08**	**0.90**	**0.38**	**4.05**	**3.04**	**5.37**	**2.89**	**3.40**	**2.63**	**40.71**
1976	2.43	2.81	4.12	0.60	3.21	**0.76**	**1.20**	**1.70**	11.23	10.66	5.05	5.07	48.84
1977	5.80	10.17	5.16	3.04	2.04	3.00	0.55	4.45	2.70	5.04	7.58	6.48	56.01
1978	6.76	6.22	6.69	2.88	1.74	1.59	4.38	2.31	1.57	0.71	5.41	11.09	51.35
1979	6.69	5.11	6.74	2.77	5.06	1.07	1.78	4.98	3.20	4.16	4.47	11.22	57.25
1980	4.65	6.16	7.24	0.94	1.43	4.56	3.72	5.01	4.33	6.88	7.39	5.68	57.99
1981	2.04	3.23	12.49	1.98	6.28	2.37	1.71	1.14	11.15	7.58	5.35	6.05	61.68
1982	9.22	3.98	7.63	1.88	1.73	6.15	1.67	4.02	7.29	8.16	9.20	7.98	68.91
1983	8.54	1.39	2.94	4.81	7.08	1.59	0.61	2.98	7.94	6.08	3.08	7.31	54.35
1984	11.61	4.03	2.20	0.24	1.27	1.74	0.62	2.47	5.26	8.10	9.77	5.27	52.58
1985	4.95	1.84	4.55	4.83	3.35	5.18	2.78	6.78	2.30	5.21	3.54	10.58	55.89
1986	7.35	0.25	3.96	4.64	5.74	3.06	2.55	6.97	0.80	6.82	9.39	9.59	61.12
1987	1.14	4.82	5.34	4.63	1.20	4.58	2.80	1.05	4.45	9.88	4.62	6.92	51.43
1988	10.15	4.65	5.96	2.14	5.47	1.01	6.70	6.41	3.27	4.25	2.13	2.10	54.24
1989	3.31	8.61	7.45	3.78	0.39	1.67	3.10	2.39	2.60	7.09	3.51	8.51	52.41
1990	11.59	12.84	1.58	1.00	0.91	5.13	2.20	1.64	2.73	6.03	3.97	5.77	55.39
1991	8.60	4.29	6.12	5.30	0.53	4.96	4.39	1.73	5.08	7.49	6.89	2.11	61.15
1992	3.19	3.09	4.47	4.19	2.91	2.02	4.25	11.04	6.07	3.96	13.48	8.10	66.77
1993	12.61	0.54	0.58	7.66	4.47	3.14	5.08	1.86	7.16	5.08	3.97	14.68	66.83
1994	**10.62**	**7.39**	**8.33**	**5.11**	**5.51**	**2.91**	**2.53**	**3.22**	**5.27**	**6.46**	**7.90**	**14.04**	**79.29**
1995	13.05	9.32	3.83	1.63	3.64	0.56	2.84	1.13	6.06	7.70	7.86	5.45	63.07
1996	6.49	7.24	4.47	3.10	6.13	1.73	1.92	4.39	2.93	9.89	8.77	2.53	59.59
1997	1.01	14.40	2.69	1.20	5.79	**6.14**	**3.74**	**8.44**	2.96	4.35	9.17	9.04	68.93
1998	**10.15**	**1.70**	**9.41**	**7.91**	**1.85**	**8.18**	**3.27**	**2.10**	**5.59**	**16.84**	**6.24**	**8.45**	**81.73**
1999	14.6	3.73	3.82	6.88	4.19	3.56	1.16	7.15	10.78	4.97	5.40	11.96	78.20
2000	**4.0**	**8.50**	**2.57**	**8.93**	**4.53**	**3.47**	**2.37**	**4.02**	**7.97**	**14.41**	**13.94**	**15.17**	**89.88**

This table shows the monthly rainfall in Blackwood from 1968 to 2000. Whether or not the increase in rainfall over the period is due to global warming we do not know but it is a fact that the wettest three years in order were *2000, 1998 and 1994* while the driest were **1973, 1975** and **1969**. The driest summer was in **1976** and the wettest in **1997**; the wettest winter was the winter of **1994-95** and the driest that of **1975-76**. My thanks are due to Mr. Idwal Davies, formerly Head of Geography at Blackwood Comprehensive School, who has been kind enough to provide this data.

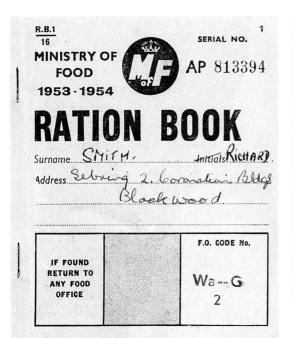

R.B.1
16

MINISTRY OF FOOD
1953-1954

AP 813394

SERIAL NO.   1

RATION BOOK

Surname SMITH.   Initials RICHARD.

Address Sebring 2. Coronation Bldgs
Blackwood

IF FOUND
RETURN TO
ANY FOOD
OFFICE

F.O. CODE No.

Wa--G
2

6 ENTER NAMES AND ADDRESSES OF RETAILERS

MEAT	(WOOD)
EGGS	(BLACKWOOD) LIMITED
FATS	F. W. MAYDWELL WOODFIELD SIDE. BLACKWOOD. MON
CHEESE	F. W. MAYDWELL, WOODFIELD SIDE. BLACKWOOD. MON
BACON	F. W. MAYDWELL WOODFIELD SIDE. BLACKWOOD MON
SUGAR	F. W. MAYDWELL WOODFIELD SIDE. BLACKWOOD. MON
SPARE	

13

R.B.1
16

TEA

If you deposit this page fill in overleaf
and on page 2.

52	50
TEA	TEA
13	13
13	13
TEA	TEA
51	49

48	46	44	42	40	38	36	34
TEA	TEA	TEA	TEA	TEA	TEA	TEA	TEA
12	12	11	11	10	10	9	9
12	12	11	11	10	10	9	9
TEA	TEA	TEA	TEA	TEA	TEA	TEA	TEA
47	45	43	41	39	37	35	33
32	30	28	26	24	22	20	18
TEA	TEA	TEA	TEA	TEA	TEA	TEA	TEA
8	8	7	7	6	6	5	5
8	8	7	7	6	6	5	5
TEA	TEA	TEA	TEA	TEA	TEA	TEA	TEA
31	29	27	25	23	21	19	17
16	14	12	10	8	6	4	2
TEA	TEA	TEA	TEA	TEA	TEA	TEA	TEA
4	4	3	3	2	2	1	1
4	4	3	3	2	2	1	1
TEA	TEA	TEA	TEA	TEA	TEA	TEA	TEA
15	13	11	9	7	5	3	1

R.B.11   **PERSONAL POINTS (SWEETS)**   21
16

Food Office Code No. as on front cover

Surname and Initials...
This page may be detached and used by itself but, if you do detach it, you should fill in details above.

E6	E6	E6	E6	D6	D6	D6	D6
E5	E5	E5	E5	D5	D5	D5	D5
E4	E4	E4	E4	D4	D4	D4	D4
E3	E3	E3	E3	D3	D3	D3	D3
E2	E2	E2	E2	D2	D2	D2	D2
E1	E1	E1	E1	D1	D1	D1	D1

158. Throughout the 1939-45 War and for a significant time afterwards, food and other essential items such as clothes, furniture and petrol were rationed. This page shows the front and three inside pages of a Ration Book for the year 1953-54 some nine years after the end of the war. Every person needed to be registered with a retailer for such foodstuffs as Meat, Eggs, Fats, Cheese, Bacon and Sugar. The double-sided page of Tea coupons shows coupons numbered from 1 to 52, one for each week of the year. To buy sweets we had to use Personal Points which could be detached and spent anywhere.

159. Virtually everyone who lived in the Sirhowy Valley in the 1970s would have been aware that Berwyn Price was a gold medal winner at the Commonwealth Games but very few are aware that Blackwood had had a gold medal winner before that. In the last British Empire and Commonwealth Games, held at Cardiff in 1958, Penry Morgan won a gold medal for racing and showing pigeons. Penry is shown here with Red King, one of his greatest pigeons. A founder member of the local pigeon club, which had its first meeting at the Mason's Arms in 1921, Penry had many important triumphs, wins at Berwick and Perth being considered his greatest. Apart from breeding, showing and racing pigeons Penry was much sought after as a judge, the highlight of his judging career being asked to adjudicate at the world-famous Cork show in 1958.

160. The gold medal won by Penry Morgan with his prize pigeon at the British and Commonwealth Games at Cardiff in 1958.

161. Staff at Cwmfelinfach Junior School celebrating Red Nose Day as part of their contribution to Comic relief: Sue Nicholls, Patience Cobley, Tina Williams, Carol Brodley and Judith Hill.

162. A group of employees from Oakdale Colliery on a trip to the Wye Valley in 1960. They include: Jack Uren, Bernard Williams, John Boxham, Clive, Tom Williams, George Windsor, John Smallcombe, Sonny Morris, Bill Williams, Jack Badham, Ron Radford, Bill 'Pitman', Gwilym Jones, Bill, Twink, Derek Williams, Joe Oliver, Bernard Daniels, Clive Fairclough, Doc Rees, Les Williams and Jimmy Cordell.

163. Councillor Tom Williams presenting John Giles with a plate to mark the occasion of Islwyn Borough Council taking over responsibility for The Miners' Institute, Blackwood on 5 December 1990. Also in the photograph are John Elston, Ken Morgan, Kevin Webb and Brian Sterry.

164. There was a thriving youth group at Mount Pleasant Baptist Church in the late 1940s and early 50s. Some fifty years later (5th August 1998) they gathered at Maes Manor, together with their spouses, for a first reunion. From the left: Peter Jones, Avril Morgan, Gwyneth Jones (Evans), Brian Mantle, Harold Fozzard, Clive Saunders, Edna Fozzard (Owen), Clive Rogers, Dorothea Saunders (Lewis), Gwilym Walker, Ewart Smith, June Mantle (Beard), Patrick Hodges, Betty Smith, Mary-Lynne Parfitt (Jones), Pat Jenkins, Marjorie Howden (Hughes), Alan Rees, Graham Walker, Shirley Rees (Jenkins), Betty Riley, Valerie Harrison (Hughes), Jill Walker, Mary Jinks, (Harris), Owen Parfitt, Keith James, Grace Hodges (Savigar), Barbara Gerrett, Barbara Church (Granville), Clive Lewis, Glenys Kukurudz (Norman), Jill Morgan (James), Bronwen Martin (Church), Valmai Stevens (Norman), Glenys James, Vivian Martin, John James, Ralph Stevens, Arthur Jenkins, Wally Kukurudz, Brian Gerrett, Kinsley Church.
(Names in brackets are maiden names)

165. A party from Stanley Street on a day trip c1950. Back: Albert Meek, Gordon Rosser, Gary Rosser, Percy Meek, Stan Lewis. Standing: Sidney Davies, Joyce Lewis, Mrs. Lewis, Mrs. Gorse, Mrs. Bickley (Senior), Mr. and Mrs. Reg Davies, Mrs. Rosser, Mrs. Gore, Mrs. Meek, Mrs. Lewis, Mr. and Mrs. Bickley, Mrs. Dodd. Front Row: Mr. Lewis, June Gore, Sheila Davies, Pat Luck, Beryl Lewis, George Gore, Tony Gore, John Lewis, Joan Bickley, Davies, Dorothy Lewis.

166. A charity event held at Blackwood Junior School c1940 to raise money for Dr. Barnados. Included in the group are: Marjorie Bennett, Agnes Brown, Alice Edwards, Joan Evans, Valerie Gibbs, Donald Hughes, Mabel Hunt, Maureen Hunt, Noreen Jones, Sylvia Morgan, Pat Sage, Grace Savigar, John Smallcombe, Joan Lewis.

167. Oakdale cooking staff around the time of the 1926 strike. Their menu is quite basic but must have been most acceptable under the circumstances: Roast Beef followed by Plum Pudding.

168. In November 1983 the fourth birthday of the founding of the 2nd Blackwood Boys' Brigade Company, based at the Central Methodist Church, coincided with the centenary of the founding of the Boys' Brigade in this country. The officers, celebrating here with their charges, are: (on the left) Glenys Smallman, Keith Smallman, Sherry Williams, David Holding, Gordon Williams and (on the right) Stuart James, Ray Holding, Marjorie Holding, Janet Horler.

169. The team of runners from the 2nd Company Blackwood Boys' Brigade who competed in the Centenary Run at Newport in June 1983. The company was based at the Central Methodist Church and are pictured here outside the Islwyn Borough Council Offices, Pontllanfraith, before leaving for the competition. Standing: Martin Williams, Darran James, Tim Silcocks, Stephen Horler, Simon MacCracken, Darren Morris. In front: David Morgan, Andrew Royall, Anthony Hilditch, Leigh Thomas, Christopher Hopkins.

170. Pontllanfraith Probus Club was established by members of Pontllanfraith Rotary Club in 1992. It is a club for retired or partially retired professional and business men and meets on the second Thursday of each month at Maes Manor Hotel. This picture shows the members who visited the Morgan Car Plant at Malvern on 8th August 1995. Elwyn West (President 1992-1994), Peter Downing, Finlay Beaton, Ken Evans, John Coker (President 1999-2000), Terry Maslen, Ron Owens, Richard Morgan (President 1995-96), Jack Davies (President 2000-01), Selwyn Lewis (Secretary 1997 to date), our Morgan guide, Colin Donovan (Secretary 1994- 97), Mervyn Price, Ray Young, Ewart Smith (President 1994-95).

171. A ladies' group from Markham who visited the Houses of Parliament c1958. They are shown here with our local member of parliament Harold Finch and his wife (on his right).

172. This photograph taken in Blackwood tells us a lot about the life of women in the 1920s. It was taken on a Monday morning at the rear of Woodward's shop in the High Street. Emily Cuzner is part of the way through the weekly wash. It is dry so she is able to do the washing outside. A chair has been taken from the kitchen and the tin bath has come down from its place on an outside wall. Water has been boiled in a large saucepan on the blackleaded range or open fire and carried outside to add to water already in the bath. Using the zinc rubbing board and a large block of Puritan soap the week's wash is progressing. Each article is washed separately then placed in the basket on the ground. From here it will be carried to the mangle, put through it and then pegged out to dry. If you think this was hard work imagine what it was like on a wet day. Then the washing took place inside the house; in the kitchen or scullery. If it was impossible to dry the wet clothes outside they would be dried inside either on a clothes-horse in front of the open coal fire or on a wooden grid which could be lowered by a pulley system then raised almost to the ceiling. When the clothes were dry enough to press a large flat iron was used. It was heated in the fire and clipped on to a flat tray. The damp clothes could then be ironed and would remain clean.

The background shows a house so typical of these parts at the beginning of the twentieth century. The sash windows are set in a wooden frame surrounded by local brick; the main wall being roughly hewn stone from a local quarry laid in black mortar. In the window stands an aspidistra - an Asian plant of the lily family with long tough evergreen leaves and small brownish flowers - a plant which no home could be without. The unpaid housewife was frequently short of money and even the most industrious found it difficult to keep their home clean and tidy. There was always coal dust in the air and there were the filthy clothes brought home every day by the collier who bathed in front of the fire. Most meals were prepared from basic ingredients - bread, tea, butter, milk, cheese, porridge and bacon. Tasty extras were mainly homemade - jam, pickles, chutney and soft fruit which had been preserved in kilner jars.

Looking at this photograph sets one wondering as to how women spent the rest of their waking time. Apart from the war period (1914 to 1918), when women were employed in factories and generally replacing the men who went to serve in the forces, women had little option other than to look after their families. Boys were trained for paid work but for girls the only preparation was for domestic work. Their education was therefore geared towards learning how to be good mothers and homemakers. They were taught how to cook, sew, launder and look after children. In this valley, the available employment was almost exclusively in the heavy manufacturing and extractive industries, that is, it was employment for men. About the only employment for women was domestic service or shop work. Life has changed a lot for everybody since those days, particularly for women.

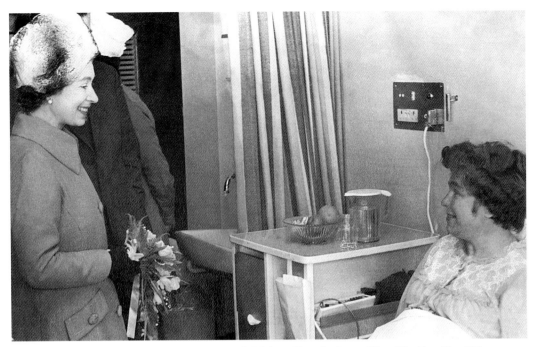

173. The £20 million University of Wales Hospital at The Heath, Cardiff, was officially opened by the Queen, accompanied by Prince Philip, on Friday 19 November 1971. This picture shows the Queen chatting with Mrs. Jean Morgan of Penllwyn, Blackwood, as she did a tour of the hospital after the opening. The Royal couple commented on the amount of modern technology that surrounded Mrs. Morgan which included push-button radio and an intercom system. It is easy to forget how much things have advanced over the space of three decades.

174. Charles Morgan, in 1953, at his Twyn Glas Bungalow on Bryn Road with his new Bentley automatic. It was believed to be the first such car in the area.

175. George Head at his last. In the late 1920s and early 1930s George Head, a local shoemaker, was also the local news gatherer for the Argus. Apart from the news of the time he wrote a series of Reminiscences under the name of Pen. Some of these shed considerable light on prominent local people and on life in Blackwood in the late 1800s. For example there was Lucy Parker, who with her husband George, kept a sweet and green-grocery business on the present site of Shaws the draper. Behind the shop they had a bakery and on the opposite side of the High Street was the principal water supply of the village. It was known to all as Lucy Parker's spout.

In those days the housewife baked her own bread in an oven at her own fireside, but those who had no oven baked their bread in George Parker's. Once every year, on Whit Sunday, the children of the Sunday-schools were given a meal of tea, cake and bread and butter, and it was at the bakehouse of George Parker that the women of the churches made the cake and bread.

I have a clear recollection (writes George Head) of going to that old bakehouse with my mother, when a boy of five or six, the ladies with Lucy Parker made the cake and bread and George Parker baked it.

George continues *'Lucy Parker was widely known in the district for the delicious toffee she made. As a boy I was greatly interested in watching her boil the sugar, and at boiling point pour it out of a large saucepan on to a large, clean and well-buttered stone. She made the toffee into long skeins, and after rolling them on the stone, cut them with a scissors into square pieces about half an inch in length. Lucy Parker's toffee - and particularly that flavoured with peppermint - was a household word, and scores of people called at the shop every Saturday evening to make purchases, many of them to enjoy the toffee while they sat through the sermon at their chapel on Sunday. But Lucy Parker was better known as a midwife than a toffee maker. Babies came regularly into the homes of most people, and her services were much in demand. Many of the women were in poor circumstances, but it made no difference. Lucy Parker went willingly when called at any time during the day or night, without any thought of payment. She was loved by the mothers of Blackwood in those days as no other woman was, and the children grew up to revere her. At childbirth and at times of sickness in the home, Lucy Parker was always present, and her presence shed a radiance of sweetness and light. Everything she said or did was graceful, kind and gentle. She was always happy in thought and feeling, and she made everybody happy with whom she came in contact.'* What a wonderful woman Lucy Parker must have been.

176. The participants in a pageant at Pentwyn Road School, Blackwood c1910. The headmaster is Mr. Hough.

177. Senior girls of the 1st Blackwood Girls' Brigade, Central Methodist Church in the Spring of 1981. They are displaying the results of a sponsored 'knit-in' for charity.

178. Duke of Edinburgh Award Winners of the 1st Blackwood Girls' Brigade with County Councillor Doug Bosley and Mrs. Bosley after their presentations in 1982: The girls are Audra Burton, Rhiannon Head, Deborah Burton, Sarah Wyatt, Alison Hopkins, Karen Spillet.

179. Oakdale Youth Choir, Musical Director Nigel Jones, Accompanist David Blackwell, performing at the Llangollen International Musical Eisteddfod in 1990 where they were awarded Second Prize. Back row: Timothy Hughes, Daniel Brake, Brian Froude, Lee Skelton, Robert Bourton, Andrew Froude, Jared Davies, Richard Newbury, Christopher Newbury, David Lawrence, Jonathan Newbury. Middle row: Helen Cormie, Angela Jones, Rebecca Mann, Rachael Hopkins, Natalie Beddoes, Debra Morgans, Amanda Thomas, Alison Humphries, Heidi Fletcher, Susan Coombes, Joanne Lloyd. Front row: Lisa Thomas, Katrina Beacham, Elizabeth Coombes, Joanna Roper, Jill Padfield, Sarah Rees, Emma Knight, Hayley Smith, Donna Probyn. The choir was formed in 1985 following a highly acclaimed Oakdale Comprehensive School production of 'Jesus Christ Superstar'. Pupils who were due to leave school suggested to Nigel Jones, Head of Music, that a Youth Choir be formed comprising past and present pupils. The choir soon became established and gained a reputation for the excellence of its musical standards. Many first prizes were won at local competitions particularly at the Miners' Eisteddfod at Porthcawl. They were semi-finalists in Sainbury's 'Choir of the Year' in 1986; competed in several international competitions and made a successful tour to the United States. The choir disbanded in 1996 after twelve successful years of music making.

180. Dr. Mackay at a Pontllanfraith Auto Club's Annual Dinner in the 1950s presenting the Dr. Mackay Cup to John Roberts as winner of the 350cc Cyril Morgan Time Trial. Dr. Mackay was a highly respected and accomplished doctor who lived at Pontllanfraith and had a surgery on Blackwood Road.

181. Children of Glen View, Caerllwyn Terrace and Greenfield Terrace, Ynysddu celebrating VE Day in 1945. Back row: Joan Roberts, Daphne Jones, Doreen Adams, Grace Miller, Joan Roberts, Ray Adams, Peter Jones, Roy Box. Third row: Keith Ivings, Venmore Roberts, Brian Jones, Michael Barnett, unknown, David Prosser, John Miller, David Games. Second row: Unknown, Jane Ivings, Nancy Prosser, Unknown, Marjorie Lewis, Dennis Roberts, Sylvia Williams, Thomas Prosser, others unknown. Front row: Valerie Jones, Sheila Thomas, Irene Thomas, Pam Jones, unknown, Gwyneth Nutland, Jackie Barnett, next three unknown, Diane Ivings, unknown. Front left: Edna Roberts, unknown.

182. A group of adults from Glen View, Caerllwyn Terrace and Greenfield Terrace, Ynysddu celebrating VE Day 1945. They include - in the back row: Rae Barnett, Vicar Andrews, Mr. Lewis, Tommy Prosser, Cyril Barnett, Mr. Games. Middle group: Bridget Collins, Mrs. Lewis, Mrs. Bryant. Front group: Eileen Berry, Mrs. Thomas, Mrs. Prosser, Lucey Berry, Jessie Jones, Mrs. Games, Mrs. Berry.

183. Principals in Blackwood Operatic Society's production of Viva Mexico in 1979. Back row: Reg Nash, Monica Harris, Huw Jones. Front row: Trevor Trace, Eluned Davies, Beverley Knight, Tom Powell, Joan Williams, Evelyn Chant, Elfed Morgan. On stage: Glyn Bebb, Anita George.

184. Bass members of the chorus in Blackwood Operatic Society's production of The Mikado staged at the Miners' Welfare Hall in 1960. Standing: Sid Morgan, Redvers Parfitt, Ron Hamer, Gordon Hart, Ron Radford, George Harris. Seated: John Goodwin, Garfield Parfitt, Len Hill, Roley Parfitt.

185. Mynyddislwyn Male Voice Choir 1971-72.

The front row includes Mrs. Grant (Musical Director centre), Ralph Walker (Deputy Musical Director), Idris Parfitt (Chairman), Mrs. Doris Swidenbank (Accompanist on right) and Mrs. Thomas (Accompanist on left).

186. Don Hendy conducting Markham Colliery Brass Band on the stage of the Royal Albert Hall, London c1972 when they were one of the twenty-four bands from all parts of the country competing for the Champion Band of Great Britain. Don Hendy had two periods as conductor of the band, the first was a thirteen year stretch in which he took them from the Second Section to Championship status and again, after a five year gap, when the band were once more promoted from the Second Section to the Champion Section. The players are - furthest row: Gwyn Evans, Michael Powell, Meirion Davies, Allen Coates, Spencer Head, Gareth Morgan. In front of these: Terry Cornish, Tom Pritchard, Gerry Price, Peter Roberts, Doug Davies. Row in front of conductor: John Evans, Chris Powell, Hedley Morgan. Sitting behind them: David Hamer, Gordon Cole, Wyndham Charles, Les Jones. Behind them, nearest camera: Ron Kelly, Tom Preece, Howard Thomas, William Hamer. On the left: Brian Reynolds, Ron Simmonds, Edward Kelly. The percussionist was Ron Jenkins who is out of the frame.

Markham and District Colliery Brass band was born as Markham British Legion Band in 1928, changing to its present name in 1930. Its activities lapsed during World War Two and it was a long time after the war before it got going again. Under Don Hendy the band reached Championship standard in 1958, moved to its own band room in 1967 and was Champion Band of Wales in 1968.

In the late 1920s, after all their music and uniforms had been destroyed in a freak storm, a Junior Band was formed at Blackwood. Both the junior and senior bands grew in stature, subsequently moving to their own purpose-built band room at the Showfield, Blackwood. The band meets for practice on Monday and Thursday evenings where they rehearse under the baton of professional musician Nigel Seaman who was a member of the National Orchestra of Wales. In 1999 the band won second prize in the Miners' National Brass Band competition and hope to be promoted to Championship status again in the not too distant future.

187. Corporal Samuel Meekosha as a young soldier.

VCs are few and far between but we are privileged to have had one living in our area. Corporal Samuel Meekosha was born in Yorkshire in September 1893. His father, Alexander, was a tailor who had emigrated from Poland and married a local girl - Mary Cunningham. Samuel enlisted in the 1/6th West Yorkshire Regiment on 20 February 1915 and was awarded his Victoria Cross for action near Yser, France on 19 November 1915. The citation, dated 22 January 1916 states *'For most conspicuous bravery near Yser on 19th November 1915. He was with a platoon of about twenty non-commissioned officers and men who were holding an isolated trench. During a heavy bombardment by the enemy, six of the platoon were killed and seven wounded, while all the remainder were more or less buried. When the senior NCOs had been either killed or wounded, Corporal Meekosha at once took command, sent a runner for assistance, and in spite of no less than ten more shells falling within twenty yards of him continued to dig out the wounded and buried men in full view of the enemy and at close range from the German trenches. By his prompt and magnificent courage and determination he saved at least four lives.'* Corporal Meekosha was decorated with his Victoria Cross by H.M. King George V at Buckingham Palace on 4th March 1916. Corporal Meekosha rose to the rank of Captain by 1920 when he was retired. During the 1930s he was a South Wales sales representative for John Player and Sons, but when World War II broke out served his country again being commissioned into the Royal Army Ordnance Corps on 15 January 1940. By the time he was discharged from the Reserve of Officers in October 1948 he had risen to the rank of Major. It is possible that the locals found his name difficult to remember and pronounce for he changed his name in 1941 from Meekosha to Ingham, the latter part of his mother's maiden name. Major Ingham's other medals were: 1914-18 Star, British War Medal, Victory Medal, Coronation Medal 1937, Defence Medal and the British War Medal 1939-45. During

188. Major Ingham in retirement.

the latter part of his life Major Ingham lived at Penrhiw Villas, Oakdale. He died on 8 December 1950 and was cremated at Pontypridd. We should not forget how much we owe to those men and women who have gone before us. Corporal Meekosha's V.C. was sold to an undisclosed buyer at a Sotherby's auction in May 2001 for £101,000.

189. The headlamps of this car have been modified to meet the regulations in operation during World War II. A rectangular box, directing a pencil of light to the ground, was fitted to the off-side lamp and a circular disc with a horizontal slit covered the near-side lamp. The available light was probably less than from a good pair of sidelights today!

190. The Royal National Lifeboat Institution boat TL-02 - the *RNLI Peter and Marion Fulton* in its blue livery in Poole harbour. The naming and dedication ceremony for the boat, which cost £1,700,000 to build, took place at Poole in April 1998.

If your father was a sailor with Cunard and your mother a stewardess with the Canadian Pacific Shipping Line, the chances are high that you would want to go to sea. Such was the case for Peter Fulton. Born in Brighton, Peter's family settled in the Blackwood area in 1930. Being forced to work in Oakdale colliery from the age of 13 gave Peter an added incentive to want to go to sea. With the help of a local doctor he was freed from the Control of Engagement Order which kept him at the colliery and joined the Navy League Sea Cadet Corps where he trained as a telegraphist. By 1944 he had reached the age of maturity (18) and joined a Tank Landing Ship. It had hardly left port when it struck a mine and sank. He was rescued, re-kitted and posted to the mine-sweeper HMS Cheerful. On her he served in the North Atlantic, around Iceland and in the North Sea until the ship was mothballed in 1947, when he returned to Blackwood on compassionate grounds to work in Tom Brown's foundry. The call of the sea was too much; Peter returned to the Royal Navy serving in the Far East as a training instructor, having now qualified as a Commissioned Communications Officer.

Peter Fulton first became involved with the Royal Naval Lifeboat Institution (the RNLI) in 1973. Communications and electronic navigational equipment for the lifeboats was becoming more sophisticated, so much so, that Communications Instructions and Procedures Handbooks were needed. Peter had written numerous handbooks in the navy while belonging to the Royal Naval Reserve, and was soon eager to help the RNLI on a voluntary basis. A caravan was purchased and fitted out as a classroom. This was towed to various coastal centres around the UK and the crews from accessible lifeboat stations attended for instruction. The Royal Yacht Association also published one of Peter's books - VHF Radiotelephony for Yachtsmen. This was necessary so that yachtsmen would conform to correct radio procedures to help lifeboatmen. In all he produced fifty-two manuals and other booklets for the Royal Naval Reserve and the RNLI. As a consequence Peter was presented with the MBE by the Queen in 1977 and received a framed vellum from the RNLI in 1987. It reads *'The Committee of Management of the RNLI, desires to place on record its grateful thanks to Lieutenant Commander P M Fulton, MBE, RD*, RNR, for the support he has given to the lifeboat service over the past fifteen years. His work for the Institution has included fitting out the first two Mobile Training Units, using them to instruct lifeboat crews in radio and voice procedure and producing detailed training documents. The dedication he has shown is an outstanding example of voluntary commitment to the lifeboat service.'* It is signed by the Chairman and Director and was presented by Countess Mountbatten. Another honour was bestowed on Peter in January 1995 when he was made an Honorary Life Governor of the RNLI - the highest honour for a voluntary worker. However the ultimate honour came in April 1998 when a prototype Severn Class lifeboat, which cost £1.7 million to build, was named *RNLB Peter and Marion Fulton*. This boat was allocated to the Training Centre at Poole for training purposes. It is wonderful to think that in this consumer, grab all society there are still people such as Peter who give their time and abilities wholeheartedly in the service of others.

191. Marion Fulton 'pressing the button' to name the *RNLB Peter and Marion Fulton* in April 1998. Also in the picture are: Reverend Cecil Clark (Staff Officer (Communications)), Lieut Commander Brian Miles (Director RNLI), Air Vice Marshall Sir Jeremy Tetley, Reverend David Jones (Vicar of St Margaret's Church, Blackwood) and Lieut Commander Peter Fulton (seated)

192. Ynysddu Secondary Modern School Choir, together with their conductor and those others who trained and helped them, when they sang at the Workmen's Hall, Cwmfelinfach on the occasion of a visit by Max Boyce c1975. There were just two boys in a choir of more than fifty. The evening is remembered for some spine tingling excerpts from Joseph and His Technicolour Dreamcoat.

E R

I WISH TO MARK, BY THIS PERSONAL MESSAGE, my appreciation of the service you have rendered to your Country in 1939—

In the early days of the War you opened your door to strangers who were in need of shelter, & offered to share your home with them.

I know that to this unselfish task you have sacrificed much of your own comfort, & that it could not have been achieved without the loyal co-operation of all in your household.

By your sympathy you have earned the gratitude of those to whom you have shown hospitality, & by your readiness to serve you have helped the State in a work of great value —

Elizabeth R

Mrs. R. Harry.

193. During the dark days of World War Two tens of thousands of children were evacuated from the cities to the relative safety of the countryside. Council officials checked every home in our area taking details of the number of bedrooms in each house and the number of people living in the house. If you had a spare bedroom you were allocated an evacuee. Some time after the war was over this personal message was sent from the Queen to thank those who had looked after evacuees.

-Choosing the Baby- at ABERBARGOED

BABIES BOYS

A bit of Good Luck from

Blackwood

Blackwood

OUR ARRIVAL

Receiving a Hearty Welcome from the Inhabitants

195. Postcards such as these were often used in place of photographs. With a suitable change of name they could be used almost anywhere. The lower comic card is postmarked 1909. I don't think Blackwood was quite the place to go for a golfing holiday then!

Acknowledgements

Numerous people have helped in the production of this book, through their willingness to share their knowledge and by the provision of old photographs and memorabilia. While every effort has been made to present facts this has often been difficult. Any errors are wholly mine and for these I apologise. My grateful thanks are due to Mr. John Watkins for checking the text and to the undermentioned who kindly loaned original material, who helped to identify faces and places, and who provided dates and other interesting information: Mrs. Margaret Baker, Mr. Gordon Bennett, Mrs. Jackie Burke, Mr. Glyn Coleman, Mr. Peter Dash, Mrs. Joyce Davies, Mr. Peter Downing, Mr. Jack Edwards, Mrs. Flynn, Mrs. J.C. Francis, Mr. Peter Fulton, Mr. Doug Gilchrist, Mr. Bryan Hemmings, Mr. Don Hendy, Mrs. Marjorie Holding, Mr. Huw Jones, Mrs. Mary Jones, Mr. Nigel Jones, the officers of Mynyddislwyn Male Voice Choir, Mr. John Roberts, Mr. & Mrs. Gary Rosser, Mr. David Smith, Mr. Malcolm Thomas, Mr. Tom Morgan, Mr. Trevor Morgan, Mr. Vernon Morgan, Miss Jenny Williams and Mrs. Doreen Withey. In particular I would like to thank Mr. Gwilym Davies and Mr. Malcolm Thomas of Old Bakehouse Publications, Abertillery. They initiated the book and have kept a careful eye on its production at every stage. I must also thank all the staff at the publishers who have always been so courteous and helpful, and who made several useful suggestions. Finally I direct readers to two sources that I have found particularly relevant to my researches for this book: 1. The History of the Grammar School in Monmouthshire, Malcolm Stephens, M.A., Thesis, 1957, University of Wales. 2. The Last Rising, David J.V. Jones, University of Wales Press, 1999. The author would welcome the loan of any unpublished photographs or other material from readers which may be suitable to include in the fifth book in this series. He may be contacted through the publishers at the address given at the front of this book.

Below is a selection of further titles available. Please send stamp to the Publishers for a detailed list.

Blackwood Yesterday in Photographs — **- Book 1**
by Ewart Smith — ISBN 0 9512181 6 6
Blackwood Yesterday in Photographs — **- Book 2**
by Ewart Smith — ISBN 1 874538 65 4
Blackwood Yesterday in Photographs — **- Book 3**
by Ewart Smith — ISBN **Old**
A Portrait of Rhymney — **- Volume 1**
by Marion Evans — ISBN 0 874538 40 9
A Portrait of Rhymney — **- Volume 2**
by Marion Evans — ISBN 1 874538 70 0
A Portrait of Rhymney — **- Volume 3**
by Marion Evans — ISBN 1 874538 41 7
A Portrait of Rhymney — **- Volume 4**
by Marion Evans — ISBN 1 874538 02 6
Brynmawr, Beaufort and Blaina in Photographs — **- Volume 1**
by Malcolm Thomas — ISBN 1 874538 15 8
Brynmawr, Beaufort and Blaina in Photographs — **- Volume 2**
by Malcolm Thomas — ISBN 1 874538 26 3
Look Back at Old Abertillery — **- Volume 1**
by Malcolm Thomas and Ray Morris — ISBN 1 874538 37 9
Trinant in Photographs — **- Volume 1**
by Clive Daniels — ISBN 1 874538 80 8
Collieries of the Sirhowy Valley
by Rayner Rosser — ISBN 1 874538 01 8
The Flavour of Islwyn Remembered
by Kay Jenkins — ISBN 1 874538 06 9
Bargoed & Gilfach in Photographs — **- Volume 1**
by Paul James — ISBN 1 874538 31 X
Bargoed & Gilfach in Photographs — **- Volume 2**
by Paul James — ISBN 1 874538 07 7
A Look at Old Tredegar in Photographs — **- Volume 1**
by Philip Prosser — ISBN 0 9512181 4 X
A Look at Old Tredegar in Photographs — **- Volume 2**
by Philip Prosser — ISBN 1 874538 81 6